NEVERTHELESS

SHE LEADS

POSTCOLONIAL WOMEN'S LEADERSHIP FOR THE CHURCH

HIRHO Y. PARK
M. KATHRYN ARMISTEAD
GENERAL EDITORS

HIGHER EDUCATION & MINISTRY
General Board of Higher Education and Ministry
THE UNITED METHODIST CHURCH

Nevertheless She Leads: Postcolonial Women's Leadership for the Church

The General Board of Higher Education and Ministry leads and serves The United Methodist Church in the recruitment, preparation, nurture, education, and support of Christian leaders—lay and clergy—for the work of making disciples of Jesus Christ for the transformation of the world. Its vision is that a new generation of Christian leaders will commit boldly to Jesus Christ and be characterized by intellectual excellence, moral integrity, spiritual courage, and holiness of heart and life. The General Board of Higher Education and Ministry of The United Methodist Church serves as an advocate for the intellectual life of the church. The Board's mission embodies the Wesleyan tradition of commitment to the education of laypersons and ordained persons by providing access to higher education for all persons.

Nevertheless She Leads: Postcolonial Women's Leadership for the Church

HIGHER EDUCATION & MINISTRY
General Board of Higher Education and Ministry
THE UNITED METHODIST CHURCH

Contents

Contents

PART 2. WOMEN ARE THE CHURCH

PART 3. WOMEN WILL BE THE CHURCH

Introduction

Rev. Dr. HiRho Park, Vice President for International Relations and Advancement, Huree University, Ulaanbaatar, Mongolia

---

Be still, and know that I am God!

—Psalm 46:10 (NRSV)

Women have been the church, women are the church, and women will be the church.

In 2020, the United States commemorates the centennial of the Nineteenth Amendment of the Constitution, which gave voting rights to women. In 2016, The United Methodist Church celebrated the sixtieth anniversary of its granting full clergy rights to women. Today, about fifteen thousand clergywomen are serving The United Methodist Church worldwide.

Historically, female voices have remained isolated in the church and theological world. However, women have proven their ability to lead as clergywomen and constructive theologians. While their leadership practices sometimes challenge traditional leadership assumptions that seek to justify male dominance and female subordination, women leaders

1

are called to interrogate and deconstruct patriarchal gender paradigms. We see that clergywomen lead in spite of oppressive economic structures and power dynamics within and outside of the worldwide church.

The goal of this book is to establish an equal and just leadership paradigm for all people, especially women within the church, from a postcolonial global perspective. Toward that end, we will explore diverse United Methodist clergywomen's leadership styles and contributions. Through their stories, the writers of this book, who are all women, will demonstrate how the church may be a site of women's empowerment by providing healing and redemptive hope for a new era of justice and peace.

First, we will review from a historical perspective how The United Methodist Church has advocated for leadership, including women's leadership. The denomination has conscientiously provided space for women to envision, articulate, and participate in leading the church and society. Starting with twenty-seven Methodist clergywomen who received full clergy rights in 1956, the number of United Methodist clergywomen in the United States grew to 54,474 (11,388 active and 2,525 retired) in 2016. They constitute 27 percent of all United Methodist clergy in the United States. The number of young clergywomen is also rising. Six percent of United Methodist elders are under age thirty-five and 39 percent of them are female. However, among the sixty-six active United Methodist bishops, only seventeen are women—even though the majority of United Methodists are women.

Beginning in 2011, The United Methodist Church began to empower women leaders throughout the world—in such places as Africa, Asia, Europe and Eurasia, and Latin America—by assisting them in the organization of their own leadership development conferences. These gatherings transformed women's leadership in their settings by amplifying their voices as they challenged misogyny within the church. Women leaders around the world have confronted the ways in which The United Methodist Church reflects the grand narratives of leadership from Western and male dominant perspectives from the United States. The shadows of colonial culture, institutional ideologies, and imperialism still hang over the marginalized, especially racial-ethnic women and the LGBTQAI+ community in a postcolonial world. Hee An Choi, a professor at Boston University School of Theology, asserts:

> The power of postcolonialism that people exercise is the power of resistance and challenge. It resists the colonial and postcolonial power structures and challenges their impacts on toxic postcolonial, sociocultural, and political manipulations and institutional ideologies.[1]

The authors of this book have done exactly what Choi explained: they exemplify how a postcolonial perspective can change the paradigm of colonial discourse on leadership by challenging racism, sexism, classism, and discrimination within the church, and then hopefully will spill over into the broader society. Readers will be inspired by how these women deconstruct cultural identity, gender, representation, sexuality, and ethnicity and reconstruct what it means to lead as women. Shehla Burney reminds us how lived

---

1   Hee An Choi, *A Postcolonial Self: Korean Immigrant Theology and Church* (Albany, NY: State University of New York Press, 2015), p. 3. Kindle Edition.

experience is a critical component of postcolonial theory.[2] Sharing their lived experience, the authors demonstrate how they have emerged as strong, intellectual, and dynamic leaders amid sociopolitical subjugation and covert and overt oppression within the church.

Women's leadership in a postcolonial world intertwines with the realization of the impact of imperial dominance with the negotiation of women's voices, explorations of hybrid identity, and introductions of unconventional ways of leading people by challenging stereotypes of women and the marginalized.

From the first section, "Women Have Been the Church," readers will learn about communities that have a long history of organized women's ministry.

M. Kathryn Armistead reminds readers that women are called to be leaders of the church. She offers a practical theology of leadership and shows how ministry can be fruitful and resilient for all people, based on the biblical foundation of covenant relationship with God and following and responding to God's grace.

Cristian De La Rosa shares her experience as a Latina leader in the United States context. She portrays the leadership style of Latina women as being flexible living bridges between spaces of tension and flux and facilitating border crossing.

"When you are considered a stranger, you are pushed from the center to the margin," says **Youngsook Charlene Kang**. As a person living on the margin, she describes how

---

2   Shehla Burney, *Pedagogy of the Other: Edward Said, Postcolonial Theory, and Strategies for Critique* (New York: Peter Lang Inc., 2012).

4

she has been called by God to lead from a "hyphenated" identity in a multicultural context.

Retired **Bishop Rosemarie Wenner** relates how Methodist lay women and clergywomen have been leading the way for equal rights and full gender inclusion in Germany. Wenner reminds us that inclusion of women on all levels of leadership is more than a justice issue; it is about becoming who we are called to be as women.

In her chapter, "Leading from the Heart," **Ouida Lee** unpacks the meaning of servant leadership and says that the concept has been misunderstood and misapplied in the church, leading many to see it as weakness rather than a strength deserving respect.

In the second section, "Women Are the Church," readers will learn about communities in which women's leadership is growing exponentially.

Motoe Yamada Foor affirms that "God uses every one of us," even a Japanese-American woman who did not speak English well. Foor tells how she led as a young Christian and testifies that the current and future church cannot stand without women.

Beginning with the biblical story of the Exodus, **Connie Semy P. Mella** says that the role of women leaders can be living and giving to the church and world as they transform, enable, and disciple people of faith, particularly through education.

In the third section, "Women Will Be the Church," the authors imagine the future of emerging churches led by women.

Alka Lyall, an Indian-American, recounts her journey of finding authentic Christian faith and leadership amid plural cultural diversity in India, where women are less valued. Lyall shares the wisdom she learned from her journey. Through it all, she maintains "love the people" as the principle of her leadership.

As the first bishop elected representing the LGBTQAI+ community, **Bishop Karen P. Oliveto** refers back to 1732, when John Wesley freed a gay man from prison. She teaches readers about historical and varying cultural understandings of homosexuality and how the church may genuinely serve LGBTQAI+ people.

Through stories of Native American women and girls, **Anita Phillips** tells how Native American women's wisdom has contributed to effective church leadership. She also calls for action to eliminate all forms of human bondage that would remind us that the majority of Indigenous Peoples are still living under the tenets of colonialism.

Practicing ministry as a deacon, **Victoria Rebeck** shows how the order of deacon has been misunderstood by The United Methodist Church in its failure to recognize how God has called deacons to lead the church as ordained clergy with a different, but complementary, ministry focus than elders have. Rebeck especially raises an essential issue of how women can support fellow women in leadership.

Nevertheless, through the "dangers, toils, and snares"[3] of ministry, women lead.

---

3 Lyrics from the familiar hymn "Amazing Grace" by John Newton (1779).

PART 1

WOMEN
HAVE BEEN
THE CHURCH

God Calls Us Leaders
A Practical Theology of Leadership

Rev. Dr. M. Kathryn Armistead, PhD, Publisher, General Board of Higher Education and Ministry, The United Methodist Church

---

Do nothing from selfish ambition or conceit,
but in humility regard others as better than yourselves.
—Philippians 2:3 (NRSV)

We Are Called

Christian leaders are called by God to step out, step up, and step into a conventual relationship with God. As ordained clergy, we are leaders set apart to shepherd the Church, the Body of Christ. We are called to work with other clergy and laity to recruit, nurture, interpret, and advocate for the corporate witness of the community of faith, helping others discover, claim, and flourish in their call as future leaders. On the road to perfection, like the Good Shepherd we follow, we do not leave anyone behind. We are called to be like Abraham—called to go and blessed to be a blessing. We are called to be like Deborah—called to give guidance and dispense justice—and like Esther, whose witness was "for such a time as this." And foremost, our covenant calls for a corporate witness to imitate and follow our Lord and Savior Jesus Christ, wherever he leads.

Ironic as it may sound, Christian leadership begins with a covenant to lead by following and responding to God's grace as members of the global Church, the Body of Christ. And just as Jesus turned the world upside down, into a place where the least, last, and lost have seats at the heavenly banquet, where a woman became the first evangelist,[1] where women became the first witnesses of the Resurrection,[2] where the last become first and the first become last, he also turned what we know as leadership upside down. Therefore we are freed for joyful obedience, and, in response, we commit ourselves to go into the world to preach and teach all nations—to make disciples to transform the world.[3]

All Christians are claimed by God. That fact is symbolized through the sacrament of baptism, in which God brings us into a covenantal relationship. And as we grow and become more firmly rooted in the faith, God invites us into ministry, sometimes because of and sometimes despite ourselves. We, then, as children of God, begin a process of discernment to explore the meaning and shape of our call and learn how to live our covenant in our context. But no matter whether one is called into ordained or lay leadership, in the Methodist tradition, that call is affirmed by the Church.

Any thinking about Christian leadership, and Wesleyan leadership in particular, must begin with whom we follow—God as incarnate in Christ—and how our lives (both individually and corporately) can better conform to God's image. This theology of leadership is premised on the Trinitarian

---

1   John 4.
2   Mark 16.
3   Matt. 28:19-20.

notion that leaders, all of us, are able to respond—we are response-able—to God's grace because of God's agape love, made manifest in the redeeming power of the life, death, and resurrection of Jesus Christ and through the continued fellowship of the Holy Spirit, who sanctifies us for the hope of glory. As Randy Maddox says in his seminal work, *Responsible Grace*: "God's *grace* works powerfully, but not irresistibly, in matters of human life and salvation: thereby empowering our *response-ability*, without overriding our *responsibility*."[4] God loves us enough to offer us freedom, knowing full well that, while we may choose to follow, sometimes we chose to separate ourselves from God.

This chapter is meant to reinvigorate conversation around a theology of leadership. As such it is limited in scope and reflects the context of this writer, a United Methodist deacon who lives and works in the United States. While hopefully the views are not parochial, they are offered to help kindle more thinking about leadership and how Christian leadership is different from more secular views. Consequently, this chapter has three parts. The first part looks at how baptized believers step out to explore and claim the call to Christian leadership. This section looks at leadership as a gift given by God through the promise of covenant with God and in community. In the second part, we will see that leaders step up to learn to follow and follow to learn. This is premised on the notion that God is always doing a new thing and finding new ways to incarnate God's love. The third part discusses how leaders step in to help others flourish while maintaining their own resiliency—staying connected and helping others

---

4   Randy Maddox, *Responsible Grace: John Wesley's Practical Theology* (Nashville, TN: Kingswood Books, 1994), 55.

stay connected to the Source—and live into God's reign by keeping in view and helping God's people focus on God's redemptive shalom (peace and wholeness) for humanity and the world.

1. Nevertheless, Leaders Step Out and Claim Their Call

As a young girl, sitting through church and paying attention the entire time was difficult for me. My mind would especially wander during the sermon to distant places and dreams of what the future might hold. My parents were devout and had settled on a Methodist church because of the denomination's stance against drinking. Even as a little child, my mother, in particular, made sure that I knew stories about missionaries who risked their lives to go into distant continents and convert the peoples there. So as I sat, giving the appearance of listening, I pictured what it would be like if I was a missionary. Not many years later, I read a book about Albert Schweitzer—musician, doctor, teacher, missionary. And I thought maybe that is what God wanted for me. I was a musician, and that was where he started. Maybe.

Nevertheless despite inevitable twists and turns, those dreams of discovery never completely left. At first, I didn't understand them as a call from God, yet I knew that God was calling. My innate musical talent was good enough for me to enjoy music but not to be a professional musician. I did not become a medical doctor but became a doctor of a completely different sort, and, to date, I've not been to Africa. But I did claim my call to be a leader. I've healed people through psychotherapy, taught in various contexts, and published books to help others teach, learn, and love God with their minds in order to advance the intellectual life of a worldwide United Methodist Church.

Whether lay or clergy, we all have call stories. God's call is persistent and, if we are open to hearing, constantly present in our lives. As Bishop Kenneth Goodson preached, "When were you last called? Today!"[5] God has a purpose for each of us—a purpose that comes as a result of God's love. In the Old Testament, God's love is described as *hesed,* translated from the Hebrew as "steadfast-loving-kindness." God's love for us is so great that God is willing to covenant with us, despite our human predilections to go back on our word and break any agreement. Nevertheless, God's love is so insistent that God humbles himself and takes the part of the less power-ful.[6] As Ken Carder and Laceye Warner remind us in their book *Grace to Lead: Practicing Leadership in the Wesleyan Tradition,*[7] a call from God is a gift, not an achievement. It offers a covenantal relationship and grateful participation in God's life and mission. Yes, a call to leadership is a gift from a covenant-keeping God, but it can be a "heavy" gift with no guarantee of worldly success or accolades. Laying claim to

---

5   Thanks to Bishop Bill McAlilly for sharing this story.

6   See Genesis 15:12-21. While Abram dreams, the lamp, representing God, passes between the animal carcasses that had been cut in two. During Old Testament times, when "cutting a covenant," ratifying a treaty, the person with the lesser power walked between the carcasses, saying, in effect, to the more powerful person: "If I don't keep this agreement, so let it be done to me," i.e., cut me in two, kill me. In this scripture, God takes the part of the less powerful party and says, "So let it be done to me, if I don't keep my part of the agreement."

7   Kenneth Carder and Laceye Warner, *Grace to Lead: Practicing Leadership in the Wesleyan Tradition,* revised ed. (Nashville, TN: General Board of Higher Education and Ministry, 2016), xiv.

this heavy gift means that as leaders, we need to put away our pride and pattern ourselves after our God, who offers grace with love and humility.[8]

Jesus, who took the role of the powerless, calls us to come and follow just as he called his disciples, the men and women who served him,[9] walked with him, who were taught by him.[10] Regardless of whether our calling takes the form of a voice from heaven like Paul's, an existential crisis like Martin Luther's, a contemplative life like Teresa of Ávila's, a strangely warmed heart like John Wesley's, or a gradual realization like mine, we are nevertheless called. Our best response, then, is to go as people of grace in the assurance that we don't go alone and to know that we are equipped to lead by the power of the Holy Spirit. This approach is consonant with John Wesley's primary expectation of all leaders, that they be people of grace.

> Not only must they have an assurance of God's justifying grace, they should be actively cultivating God's sanctifying grace through spiritual disciplines and self-denial. Their character should be marked by

---

8 I say this in recognition that calls for humility, powerlessness, and service have different implications for women. See: "A Womanist Exposition of Pseudo-spirituality and the Cry of an Oppressed African Woman," by Fundiswa A. Kobo, Creative Commons Attribution License, 4/30/18, https://hts.org.za/index.php/hts/article/view/4896/11160. See also "Liberative Learning: A Look at CPE through the Lens of Black Feminist and Womanist Theology" by Danielle Buhuro, in *Reflective Practice: Formation and Supervision in Ministry*, 2016, 36:48–60. Accessed online 4/1/19.

9 Luke 8:1-3.

10 Luke 10:38-42.

an eminent measure of Christ-like love of God and neighbor, and their practice should be exemplary.[11]

To discover and claim our call, to enter into covenant, we need opportunities for discernment, safe places where we can dream the big dreams of God. We need guidance, companionship, and more experienced mentors to help light the way—in short, we need the church to embody grace and God's steadfast-loving-kindness in order to introduce us to spiritual disciplines that will nurture, educate, develop, and sustain us as leaders.

2. Nevertheless, Leaders Step Up to Follow and Follow to Learn

As humans, too often we are tossed to and fro on every wave of doctrine (Eph. 4:14). Nevertheless, to be grace-filled leaders, we need steady guidance in line with a disciplined approach to Christian spiritual practices. And we need models. In this way leaders learn to follow and follow to learn.

Just as leadership is a gift, so too are the people who mentor us and model grace, as we all serve to embody God's love for the world. I have always served beyond the local church, first as a diaconal minister and later as an ordained deacon, but I entered ministry at the time when

---

11 See: "A Wesleyan Vision for Theological Education and Leadership Formation for the 21st Century," a working document prepared by the Task Force on Theological Education and Leadership Formation, The Council of Bishops of The United Methodist Church, The United Methodist General Board of Higher Education and Ministry, and The Association of United Methodist Theological Schools, 1998, 7, https://www.gbhem.org/sites/default/files/documents/education/AWesleyanVision.pdf.

there were few women mentors. However, I was blessed to have as a mentor Betty Cloyd, a diaconal minister and, along with her husband Tom, a former missionary. But there were also outstanding lay women who had broad experience in the church. One was Thelma Stevens. I met Thelma when we were both serving on our conference Commission on the Status and Role of Women in the late 1970s. She was nearing the end of her service, while I was just beginning mine. She helped me understand how the church operated and gave me some glimpses into the inner workings and politics of the general church—blemishes and all. She was not a disillusioned idealist but a tireless advocate for social justice and civil rights. Only later did I learn the extensive impact Thelma had on the church.

We may have faithful mentors, yet we are creatures who are tied to our context in ways that are often beyond our capacity to understand—unconscious biases, unhealthy family systems, limited abilities. We all have them. Too often we also don't know how much we need God and each other. Kim Cape[12] reminds us of the words of Abba Dorotheus of Gaza, who lived in the sixth century. He wrote:

Imagine the world is a circle, that God is the center, and that the radii—the spokes—are all the different ways that human beings live. When those who wish to come closer to God walk toward the center of the circle, they come closer to each other and at the same time, they come closer to God. The closer they come

---

12 Dr. Kim Cape is the former—and first female—General Secretary of the General Board of Higher Education and Ministry, The United Methodist Church.

to God, the closer they come to one another, and the closer to one another, the closer they come to God.

Yes, we can draw closer, but even communities of faith can be like the blind leading the blind. We can be like the committee who wanted to design a horse but ended up with a camel, and we will stumble unless we keep our eyes fixed on God, who is always doing a new thing.[13] As we seek to "reform the nation, particularly the church, and to spread scriptural holiness over the land,"[14] we need leaders whose eyes are fixed on God's path, leaders who can guide and sometimes prod us to listen and stay connected to God, by keeping faith and keeping God's commandments (John 14:15). We also need leaders attuned to the new things God has in mind, ready to go and take us along.

As a called people, we are commissioned to do new things as we go in God's name together. And just as Jesus sent seventy-two disciples to go two by two into the towns and villages, leaders should not take to the road alone. And in fact, Christ has already told us where to go: "Go therefore and make disciples of all nations, baptizing them in the name of the Father and of the Son and of the Holy Spirit, and teaching them to obey everything that I have commanded you. And remember, I am with you always, to the end of the age" (Matt. 28:19-20, NRSV). Just as our call is global, our leadership must also be interculturally competent.[15]

---

13 Isa. 43:19.

14 "Minutes of Several Conversations" Q.3, in *The Works of John Wesley* [vol. 8; ed. T. Jackson; Baker, 1978], 299.

15 For intercultural competence, see HiRho Y. Park, *Develop Intercultural Competence: How to Lead Cross-Racial and Cross-Cultural Churches* (Nashville, TN: General Board of Higher Education and Ministry, 2018).

3. Nevertheless, Leaders Step in to Help Others Flourish and Live into God's Reign

Like Abraham and Sarah and all their children, leaders are blessed to be a blessing. But to stay resilient and live into the fullness of God's promise, leaders keep covenant by staying connected to God's life-giving and redemptive love, power, and justice.[16] Leadership is the most fruitful when leaders are resilient. This means taking a Sabbath and caring for one's own soul.

Knowing one's own limits and taking time away is called self-care; and pastors, in particular, don't take enough time to care for themselves. Yes, the demands of parish life are grueling and never-ending; but too often the church equates self-care with being selfish or, worse, lazy. Dr. Karen Scheib, in her book *Attend to Stories: How to Flourish in Ministry*, writes about what the bishop said at her ordination. At the end of the service the bishop recognized an annual conference leader who was stepping down from his long-time service as conference secretary. The bishop thanked the pastor for working "twelve, fourteen, eighteen hours a day." As a newly ordained elder, Karen took this to be an admonition about what was expected of her—"hard work, responsibility, being a good girl, and taking care of others."[17] The bishop's statement intersected with her own personal history to create an unsustainable story that eventually led her to leave parish ministry. It is a well-known fact that when leaders are continually stressed, tired, and overworked, they often respond in unhealthy ways—over-eating, irritability, physical illness,

---

16 See John 15:5-8.

17 Karen D. Scheib, *Attend to Stories: How to Flourish in Ministry* (Nashville, TN: Foundery Books, GBHEM Press, 2018), 13.

depression, and sometimes sexual misconduct,[18] because boundaries are more difficult to maintain. Yet, given all the evidence, self-care remains a tough sell to church leaders.

When we are healthy and resilient, our helping is more effective. However, helping others flourish has different meanings in different ministry contexts. For annual conferences, it may mean setting up accountability structures for leaders. For educational institutions, it may mean providing faculty opportunities for career advancement and achieving tenure. For chaplains, it may mean helping them learn about return on investment (ROI), so they can better express their worth in a secular setting to employers. And sometimes, for congregations, it also can mean heeding the prophetic voice of their pastor.

What do flourishing persons, congregations, and annual and jurisdictional conferences look like? There are many books on this subject, but to put it in one word, they exude peace—*shalom*, wholeness. Peace is a sure sign of flourishing.[19] Our God created us to flourish. The Hebrew word for "flourish" is *pârach*. In the Bible "flourish" is tied to blossoming, spreading forth, growing, springing up, breaking out. It is through God's grace-full covenant and only when connected to God and the faith community that we can break out, break free, and grow.

---

18 Amy Frykholm, "Fit for Ministry: Addressing the Crisis in Clergy Health," https://www.christiancentury.org/article/2012-10/fit-ministry. Accessed 9/25/18. See also research from Pulpit and Pew, http://pulpitandpew.org/which-way-clergy-health/. Accessed 9/25/18. See also A. J. Weaver, et al., "Mental Health Issues among Clergy and Other Religious Professionals: A Review of Research," *Journal of Pastoral Care and Counseling*, 2002 Winter, 56(4):393–403.

19 John 14:27-31.

But often what God intends and what happens can be two different things. In our best efforts, we may, as St. Richard of Chichester said, "love thee more dearly and follow thee more nearly"; yet our ministry may not bear all the fruit we might wish, and we can become disheartened. As a pastor, Bishop Bill McAlilly was appointed to plant a church. As you might expect, during this time, he and his team learned quite a bit. They went door to door inviting people to this new congregation, and they found that out of ten invitations, one person would say "Yes," and out of ten of those who said yes, only one would actually show up. In order to stay resilient, they counted only the "yeses."[20] To stay focused on the prize, leaders must keep their eyes on Jesus Christ, God's "Yes" for the world.[21]

What is the end-game for Christian leaders? What are the results of Christian leadership? The answer is clear. No matter where in the world leaders serve, the goal of leaders is to usher in God's Reign, God's Kingdom. And while we have faith that God makes "all things work together for good" (Rom. 8:28, NRSV), we also know that in this life we only have glimpses and foretastes of the glory to come. With this goal in mind, our job is to plant seeds.

From 2008 to 2012, Bishop Marcus Matthews was the bishop of the Upper New York Annual Conference. His assignment was to create something new in that area. He says, "It was only by God's grace that I was able to lead four Annual Conferences to become one. But this new annual conference would not have been possible except for the leadership of the four former annual conferences [that] had

---

20 Bishop Bill McAlilly, personal interview, 9/25/18.
21 See E. Stanley Jones, *The Divine Yes* (Nashville, TN: Abingdon Press, 1975).

planted seeds and birthed a plan to one day become one." Bishop Matthews goes on to say, "To sow/till means to put into the ground so that nature can do its work. For us it means as humans we can generate ideas, but it is God who makes fruit grow. These leaders of the former conferences dug deep and used good soil to plant and lay the foundation for what the area has become. We planted seeds of faith knowing that one day the harvest would come."[22]

But leaders cannot know the kind of bountiful crop that might await them—that is something that God alone can see. Debora A. Christiansen is pastor of St. Stephen United Methodist Church in Memphis, Tennessee. One day two "navigators" from Methodist Le Bonheur Healthcare knocked on the doors of the church. They had organized a group of about forty women who used the park a couple of blocks from the church for exercise. But recently they had been verbally abused by passersby and several were increasingly afraid. So the group's leaders asked Debora if they might use the church parking lot. Debora refers to this incident as a "God moment." Little did these ladies know that St. Stephen was on its way to closing its doors if something didn't happen quick.

Debora says she made a decision and said, "Yes." She knew that this was a loving, caring congregation who actively ministered to their community. Her decision was in character and in keeping with the congregation's values and practices. As she brought in the lay leadership, the church just kept saying, "Yes." "Yes, the weather is bad. Come in. You can use our fellowship hall." "Yes, you can use our kitchen for nutrition classes." "Yes, kids are welcome. We'll even start a tutoring program." "Yes, we'd be happy to host a trunk-for-treat for

---

22 Bishop Marcus Matthews, personal email, 9/19/18.

the neighborhood kids. Over 400 kids? No problem." "Yes, you are welcome to host a worship service in Spanish. We'll come and worship with you."[23]

Nevertheless, what began as the church letting a group use their parking lot has blossomed into a cornucopia of ministries that has reinvigorated St. Stephen. As the Body of Christ grows, the neighborhood people are learning to trust each other as they join together across racial and ethnic barriers to serve. The harvest is plentiful and here the workers are many. But note, it is the corporate witness of the Church that is making the difference. When the whole Body says "Yes" to God's leading, the kingdom comes into view and people flourish.

Seeing God at work gives leaders and the churches they shepherd the courage to keep going and the inspiration to keep God's commandments, including the greatest commandment. This is God's goal—for us to go and transform the world.

Keeping covenant as Christian leaders means going where God sends us and bearing the cross if called to do so. With our Christ-given, upside-down leadership model, we must put aside our desire for upward mobility, and that is hard. Being a leader doesn't mean that any of us will get rich quick or otherwise. Consequently, we subscribe to a faith community, The United Methodist Church, that will help us discern, claim, and flourish in Christ's calling. This begins with establishing pathways designed to help us discern our gifts and passions in ways that better connect us to God and to each other. It continues as the Church supports our

---

23 Rev. Debora A. Christiansen, personal communication. Used with permission.

journeys of discovery and formation and finds ways to effectively affirm our call by creating connections that will bring us closer to the hub of the wheel—God—and to each other.

Built on the bedrock of God's grace and a vision of generations of thriving, diverse, and compassionate Christian leaders to offer ministry in God's name for the Church and world, The United Methodist Church has designated the General Board of Higher Education and Ministry (GBHEM) as its leadership center for a worldwide Church. The mission of GBHEM is to build capacity for United Methodist lay and clergy leaders to discover, claim, and flourish in Christ's calling in their lives, by creating connections and providing resources to aid in recruitment, education, professional development, and spiritual formation. The United Methodist Church is here to help people as they discern and claim their call; sustain them as they explore and learn; and connect them in order to create fruitful and resilient ministry.

Conclusion

Where are leaders shining the light of Jesus? Who is fighting for the least, the last, and the lost? Who is making disciples for the transformation of the world? Those leaders who are called to step out, step up, and step in to share the Good News. We are limited and flawed; but nevertheless, God calls us leaders.

Latina Women and the Church
Mujeristas y Nepantleras

*Rev. Dr. Cristian De La Rosa, PhD, Clinical Assistant
Professor of Contextual Theology and Practice,
Boston University School of Theology*

Bridges are thresholds to other realities, archetypal, primal symbols of shifting consciousness. They are passageways, conduits, and connectors that connote transitioning, crossing borders and changing perspectives. Bridges span liminal (threshold) spaces between worlds . . .

—Gloria Anzaldúa

As a Latina clergywoman of Nahuatl descent, I find my story fittingly reflected in these words from Gloria Anzaldúa's book *This Bridge We Call Home: Radical Visions for Transformation,* where bridges symbolize a state of tension and flux, change and transformation.[1] Indeed, like most women of Latin American heritage, I experience our being and doing to be somewhat like bridges. As descendants of the

---

1   Gloria Anzaldúa and Analouise Keating, eds., *This Bridge We Call Home: Radical Visions for Transformation* (NY: Routledge, 2002), 1.

colonized, we struggle to survive within the limitations of established social systems imposed on us. We engage and facilitate justice-making processes within our communities to find spaces to exist. And we strive to connect to any expression and possibility of new life as a way to hope for, and build, a better future.

Our stories as Latina women in the church are at root about being flexible living bridges that connect different perspectives, philosophies, and peoples across geographical and chronological boundaries of cultures, traditions, and future possibilities. Sometimes we discover the bridges built by visionary Latinas who came before us. Oftentimes we find ourselves building the bridges alongside others in the community. Most of the time, however, we ourselves become the bridges that are the places or spaces for survival and transformation of our families and communities. We find ourselves in the in-between spaces facilitating border crossing.

In this chapter, I reflect on my experience as a pastor and a scholar in the context of the United States. I hope to share something about my and our struggle to survive in a state of tension and flux. I briefly communicate the particularity of my calling in the church and the academy as a product of colonization. And I conclude with reflections about how crossing borders is essential for individual and collective transformation.

The Struggle to Survive

I am originally from Mexico. I was baptized in the Catholic Church, raised as a Protestant in the context of the United States, and ordained as an elder in The United Methodist

Church. From an early age, I volunteered with different ministries in the church and learned about the impact of the gaps between our teachings and our practices. These gaps are shifting spaces that became evident to me at every level of our institutional church. I relate them to the wisdom of a saying from our Latino communities: "*Del dicho al hecho hay mucho trecho.*" This can be translated as "There is a great distance between what is said and what is done." Borrowing from the theorizing of Gloria Anzaldúa, I have come to identify these gaps between what we say and what we do in the church as my contextualized experience of *Nepantla* that most institutional leadership seems to ignore or overlook. However, these places and spaces are like home; and in some situations, it is the only home for Latina women in the church.

Nepantla is a retrieved Nahuatl word identifying the in-between of what is and what it is becoming, or hopes to be but is not at the moment: the already but not yet. I think of this conceptualization by Anzaldúa as the borderland's home of Latinas in relationship to the church. In her work, Anzaldúa notes the transformative power and vulnerability of these *Nepantla* spaces:

> Transformations occur in this in-between space, an unstable, unpredictable, precarious, always-in-transition space lacking clear boundaries. *Nepantla* es tierra desconocida [is unknown territory] and living in this liminal zone means being in a constant state of displacement—an uncomfortable, even alarming feeling. Most of us dwell in *nepantla* so much of the time it's become a sort of "home."[2]

---

2   Anzaldúa and Keating, *This Bridge We Call Home*, 1.

I believe that this *Nepantla* space within the church—gaps between our teachings or statements as a church and our practices as Christians—is the historical consequence of the colonizing processes in the Americas. In our current efforts to become an inclusive global United Methodist Church, the production and dismissal of these gaps has become one of the greatest limitations of Christianity today. The fact that Christianity was introduced by European empires as a value system supporting colonization around the world continues to problematize the mission, ministry, and practice of the church. It is difficult to forget that Christianity was imposed through a violent conquest of most of Latin America and was reintroduced as Protestantism through the expansionist ideology of Manifest Destiny across the United States.[3] Western philosophical debates questioning the humanity of native peoples, rape of indigenous women, forced conversions to Christianity, erasure of indigenous cultures and religions, plundering of wealth from the Americas, systematic appropriation of the land, and the creation of Indian reservations are still traumatic events that mark our lives and shape our identities. These are still unresolved and even ongoing issues of colonization in the Americas, Western values and processes that determined and shaped the design of present social systems and institutions.

These traumatic events left descendants of the colonized as strangers in the lands of their own ancestors. My own mestiza body reminds me of the fact that Christianity

---

3 See Luis N. Rivera, *A Violent Evangelism: The Political and Religious Conquest of the Americas* (Louisville, KY: Westminster/John Knox Press, 1992); and David A. Sanchez, *From Patmos to the Barrio: Subverting Imperial Myths* (Minneapolis: Fortress Press, 2008).

erased most Nahuatl cultural and philosophical points of reference necessary for my own existence. This reality forces me to survive in the *Nepantla* spaces of social and religious institutions where I am constantly searching for fragments of my identity—fragments and points of reference that Christianity cannot provide at this time. I inhabit the in-between spaces, an unknown shifting landscape, bridging at least two worlds of difference—the world of the colonizer that survived and thrives through globalization in a new world order at one end and the world of the colonized that struggles to survive, fragmented and invisible to most institutional processes at the other end.

Over the course of my almost thirty years of ministry, I have come to believe that it is very difficult for the church to provide meaningful and relevant points of reference for the descendants of the colonized. True, I have seen a great deal of interest and good intentions about missional priorities with diverse ethnic communities expressed by the church as an institution. And indeed, we have some interesting projects among these communities and even some leadership from ethnic communities in the upper ranks of the denomination. However, I still often walk into official church meetings today to find myself the only Latinx[4] or the only person of color in the room. Such experiences communicate that our church has not been able to see or understand the circumstances of fragmentation related to the world of the descendants of the colonized. How can the church understand that when I walk into a meeting like that I struggle to remain in

---

4   The use of "Latinx" indicates a spirit of gender inclusivity, to represent the variety of possible genders as well as those who may identify as non-gender binary or transgender. See https://www .complex.com/life/2016/04/latinx/.

the physical space and participate? How can the Christian church understand that in order for me to stay and engage such a space I am forced to consider and bridge my own fragmentation? In order to manage and survive I must draw from my indigenous roots, my imposed Mestiza culture, and my acquired Anglo Protestantism.

The struggle to survive within fragmentation is not a new conceptualization for our time. Linda Tuhiwai Smith reminds us that fragmentation "is not a phenomenon of postmodernism as many might claim. For indigenous peoples fragmentation has been the consequence of imperialism."[5] I believe I experience fragmentation as a double consequence of the Christian complicity with conquest and colonization: First, as a violent encounter that severed most of my indigenous roots when Spanish conquistadores introduced Roman Catholicism in Latin America; and second, as Protestantism from England found its way into the processes that annexed what was the north part of Mexico, now the Southwest of the United States. Protestantism was a reintroduction of Christianity that questioned the imposed Catholic version and erased much of the surviving fragments of indigenous and Mestiza cultures present in the Catholic Church.[6] In this second encounter, my family survived within the gaps of the Wesleyan tradition, where a surviving tradition of social justice and the emphasis on formation and higher education have proven to be valuable resources for my own struggle to survive.

---

5   Linda Tuhiwai Smith, *Decolonizing Methodologies: Research and Indigenous Peoples* (New York: Zed Books Ltd., 2012), 28.

6   See Nestor Medina, *Mestizaje: (Re)mapping Race, Culture, and Faith in Latina/o Catholicism* (Maryknoll, New York: Orbis Books, 2009).

In her explanation of *Mujerista* theology, Ada María Isasi-Díaz notes that "we have learned from our grand-mothers and mothers that la vida es la lucha."[7] In learning that "life is the struggle," I have come to understand that given my social location in the context of the United States there is no option about engaging the struggle for life. The only option as a Latina is where and how I struggle. Latinas survive and bridge worlds of difference to retrieve fragments of our indigenous cultures and religions in order to be and live. In the particular context of the United States we stand at the intersectionality of racist and sexist power dynamics. The privileged access I have to higher education helps me understand that surviving at these intersecting bridges is not only a struggle to survive but an action of resistance against those who would like to take yet more of my life. My ministry, like the ministry of most Latina pastors, involves the bridging of gaps between the essence of a liberating gospel that calls to life and the practices of a Christian Church that has not been able to break away from being complicit with colonial powers and ideologies. The questions of service and survival within the church continue to be a pressing matter for Latinas, particularly for Latina clergy serving within the institutional church.

Particularity of the Call to Justice Making

In preparation for ordination in The United Methodist Church, I was asked to prepare a presentation and communicate in one sentence my call to ordained ministry. My statement

---

7   Ada María Isasi-Díaz, "Mujeristas: A Name of Our Own," *The Christian Century* (1989), 106:562.

"I am called to serve God and God's people, particularly el Pueblo" generated a great deal of dialogue among the group of seminarians and clergy at the gathering. Most of the dialogue related to the second part of my statement–the particularity of my call and the use of Spanish. The responses ranged from offering English translations of "el Pueblo" to concerns about my readiness to serve and itinerate in The United Methodist Church. The particularity of my call they interpreted as a limitation to serve only with Latino congregations or with new immigrant communities in Spanish. The most interesting thing about this experience was that nobody asked me what I meant by "el Pueblo." Instead, the dialogue quickly moved to translation and accommodation within the existing possibilities and limitations of the institutional church, rather than any explanation I might offer from my own perspective.

The particularity of my call to ordained ministry is my own contextualization of the preferential option for the poor as articulated in Latin American Liberation Theology. This intersects, in the context of the United States, with the option for those who are made poor (the impoverished) as articulated by Ada María Isasi-Díaz in *Mujerista* Theology.[8] It is always difficult to translate "el Pueblo." In my conceptualization I do not translate it only as "people" or "poor people." El Pueblo is every community aware of its circumstances and collective agency. Its members struggle to survive but they are nonetheless actively involved in the struggle for their own liberation. I continue to use this statement when I am asked to speak about vocational discernment or my call to

---

8   Ada María Isasi-Díaz, *Decolonizing Epistemologies: Latina/o Theology and Philosophy* (New York: Fordham, 2012), 46–47.

ordained ministry. I always begin by explaining the meaning of "el Pueblo" and the particularity of my call as a way of framing an intentional dialogue about possibilities that considers the limitations of established institutions, epistemological retrieval from different cultures, and the agency of those who are excluded from the life, ministry, and leadership of the church or the academy today.

I believe it is from within or through the *Nepantla* spaces in the church that the most significant and relevant ministry is done by Latina women in the church. Our calling to serve as clergy is intrinsically related to our experiences of *Nepantla* in relationship with el Pueblo and our experiences of the church as an institution. It is in my favorite response of "aqui en la lucha" (here in the struggle) to the question "How are you?" that I clarify and find affirmation of the particularity of my own calling. Along the journey as clergy and as faculty at a seminary, my priority has been to identify the institutional gaps where I can survive and facilitate access and transformation. As a person of Nahuatl descent, I draw on my indigenous roots and consider that I am a *Nepantlera* as theorized by Gloria Anzaldúa. I am a dweller of *Nepantla* who facilitates border crossing at intersecting bridges where transformation is inescapable. As she explains, I am one of "those who facilitate passage between worlds, . . . with states of mind that question old ideas and beliefs, acquire new perspectives, change worldviews, and shift from one world to another."[9]

As a Mexican immigrant to the United States I draw from my imposed Mestiza culture and consider myself a *mujerista* as theorized by Ada María Isasi-Díaz. In her articulation of

---

9   Anzaldúa and Keating, *This Bridge We Call Home*, 1.

Mujerista Theology, Isasi-Díaz systematizes the particularity of the experience of Latina women. She relates the struggle, the bridge-building, and God's calling to facilitate justice-making. She explains what it means to be a *mujerista*:

> a *mujerista* is one who struggles to liberate herself, who is consecrated by God as proclaimer of the hope of her people. *Mujerista* is one who knows how to be faithful to the task of making justice and peace flourish, who opts for God's cause and the law of love. In the *mujerista* God revendicates the divine image and likeness of women. The *mujerista* is called to gestate new women and men: a strong people. *Mujeristas* are anointed by God as servants, prophets and witnesses of redemption. *Mujeristas* will echo God's reconciling love; their song will be a two-edged sword, and they will proclaim the gospel of liberation.[10]

A *mujerista* embodies the hope for a new reality of shalom (peace with justice) with an option for el Pueblo. She is consecrated by God, and in her facilitating of justice making she engages in the bridge building for the birth of a new people. This is not mere theorizing; I think here of Latinas leading ministries and congregations in the context of the United States, and this is what they do in practice. Most of us serve in relation to new immigrant communities at a time that human migration around the world is a pressing global issue. Current immigration policy in the United States alongside growing racist attitudes makes immigrant communities the most vulnerable. In response to the needs of new immigrant communities, pastoral ministry for Latinas includes

---

10 Isasi-Díaz, "Mujeristas: A Name of Our Own," 560.

translation, orientation to a new culture and social institutions, English-as-a-second-language programs, and resourcing for all the basic needs of housing, employment, and care for children. Alongside preaching and leading of worship in a local congregation, Latina pastors facilitate spaces for el Pueblo. Local congregations become community centers for new immigrant communities.

Border Crossing and Transformation

As Latina clergy, I draw from my acquired Protestantism and consider a tradition of social justice that survives as a prophetic element within The United Methodist Church (UMC). The mission, Social Principles, and *Book of Resolutions* of The UMC alongside individuals engaging the unresolved issues of colonialism serve as key points of reference resourcing my own practice of ministry.[11]

The contextualization of these resources for me involves bridge building and border crossing among the church, the community, and the academy. A ministry I have the privilege to facilitate is the Hispanic Youth Leadership Academy (HYLA), an intentional leadership formation effort with Latinx students. Its mission reflects The UMC mission—to make disciples of Jesus Christ for the transformation of the world—and relates it to el Pueblo:

> We, the Hispanic Youth Leadership Academy (HYLA), are a coalition of United Methodist Youth/Young Adult student leaders. Our mission is to discern our call to ministry through the pursuit of higher

11 See the 2016 *Book of Discipline* and *Book of Resolutions* of The United Methodist Church.

education, awareness of social issues, spiritual and mental growth, and our awakening as leaders. We develop our leadership skills as we discover our passion through practice within the United Methodist Church and our individual communities. We unite together in solidarity through our common Latin@ experience and are committed to help the Pueblo Latino regardless of legal status in order to transform the world.[12]

Latina women, particularly clergywomen, have been the church and will continue to be the church in relationship to el Pueblo and the limitations of our social location. We survive within the institutional gaps of the church as subversive acts of resistance. In our ministries we are living bridges that facilitate border crossing as essential to individual and collective transformation. Latinas in the leadership of the church are *mujeristas* and *Nepantleras,* struggling to retrieve surviving fragments of indigenous knowledge in order to become who God means for us to be—mujeres in the image of God.

---

12 See hylaumc.com. For a fuller explanation about words used to describe Latinos, see also https://link.springer.com/article /10.1057/s41276-018-0142-y.

Nevertheless, She Leads

Rev. Dr. Youngsook Charlene Kang, DMin, Mountain Sky Conference, The United Methodist Church

---

"For in the end, freedom is a personal and lonely battle,
and one faces down fears of today
so that those of tomorrow might be engaged."
—Alice Walker, *In Search of Our Mothers'
Gardens: Womanist Prose*

Living on the Margin

My story is a story of a person living on the margin. Yet in spite of and even because of my marginality, I am called to lead, and therefore I lead.

I came to the United States as a foreign student to further my graduate study in sociology. Education was an important value that I inherited from my mother. I came as a young mother traveling with our two children—ages three and one—to join my husband, who arrived one year earlier to attend seminary in Denver, Colorado. I remember that all I brought, for the three of us, was two suitcases, because I thought we would go back to Korea when we finished our studies.

Yet having now lived in the United States for more than thirty years, I still feel that I am a stranger in a strange land.[1] I still feel that I am singing the Lord's song in a foreign land.[2] But I am not alone; the experience of living on the margin is something common to ethnic minorities in this country, including Asian Americans, who often live between two cultures. It is our experience that people on the street see us as foreigners, even if we were born and raised in the United States. That reality, with which Asian Americans struggle, points to a more general attitude toward strangers. When you are considered a stranger, you are pushed from the center to the margin. You are not the norm; you are an exception. You are not seen as "typical" but seen as a special case. That is even more true if you speak with an accent. So, marginality is inherent in being a stranger. Using the term of Jung Young Lee, I as an ethnic minority woman live "in-between."[3] Even after all this time, I am a stranger living in two worlds. Although I am a US citizen, I am often seen as a foreigner or alien.

This in-between marginal experience is shared among many ethnic minority groups. Ada María Isasi-Díaz moans that she will always be a marginalized stranger, even when she returns to the city of her birth. "The marginality is within," she says.[4] Living in-between two worlds and two cultures, I

---

1   I shared a part of this story in my article "Interfaith Spirit of Justice," in *Wellsprings: A Journal of United Methodist Clergy-women*, March 2018, http://www.wellspringsjournalpodcast.org /2018/04/14/2018-creating-2/.

2   Psalm 137:4, NRSV.

3   Jung Young Lee, *Marginality: The Key to Multicultural Theology* (Minneapolis: Augsburg Fortress, 1995), 44–47.

4   Ada María Isasi-Díaz, "A Hispanic Garden in a Foreign Land," in *Inheriting Our Mothers' Gardens: Feminist Theology in Third*

often feel like I belong in neither. Likewise, when I visit South Korea, where I was born and grew up, I see people notice that I am different, and I internalize marginality as if I were born with it. The reality of living in-between is made plain in my hyphenated identity—*Korean-American*. And this context has defined my identity, life, and ministry over the last thirty-some years.

Being a Korean American Clergywoman

I happen to be one of the first-generation Korean American clergywomen in The United Methodist Church. This generation suffered from a great deal of prejudice and also had to break through the ice of discrimination against ordained women. We were persecuted simply because we were called to ORDAINED ministry. We were not to preach from the pulpit. For some, a woman's ordination was almost considered a punishable crime. Many Korean American men and women alike seemed to think that our voices needed to be muted or stifled. That was thirty years ago.

Why take such a difficult path? I am called by God. My call to ordained ministry came in August 1987, when I attended a global United Methodist clergywomen's consultation in Great Gorge, New Jersey. A Korean American friend at Iliff School of Theology "persuaded" me to attend the event. It was one month before I was going to start a dual degree program—pursuing a Master of Divinity at Iliff School of Theology and the Master of Social Work at the University of Denver. My intention was to become a social worker, even

World Perspective, Letty M. Russell, et al., eds. (Philadelphia: Westminster John Knox Press, 1988), 92.

though I was getting an MDiv degree too. This gathering of close to one thousand women changed the course of my life! During one of the worship services I felt a call of God into ordained ministry. The worship was so empowering that it was as if all who gathered were affirming my call.

I met other Korean American clergywomen for the first time there at Great Gorge. Over a dozen Korean women were present at the gathering, including a few ordained and several seminarians. After the consultation was over, the Korean women stayed for a few more days in order to hold the third National Korean American Clergywomen's gathering. This community of Korean American clergywomen was just beginning to form, and the foundation had already been laid to become a national organization. Rev. Sehee Han writes in her article on the history of Korean American Clergywomen, "It was at the second gathering of Korean American clergywomen in 1986 that the bylaws of their association were adopted. There were 10 ordained and 21 seminarians in 1986."[5]

The Korean American Clergywomen held an annual meeting every August. We gathered, worshipped, talked, cried, laughed, and played. The stories shared were different and yet familiar. There were the stories full of joys and struggles—how we were called to ministry and yet were not accepted by our own churches and communities. Our stories brought us to tears and solidarity. Thus, my ministry is a fruit of the interweaving of The United Methodist Church and the

---

5   Sehee Han, "The History of the Korean-American Clergywomen Association of The United Methodist Church, 1985-2000," in *The History of the Korean American Clergywomen of The United Methodist Church*, 15th Anniversary Celebration, The General Board of Global Ministries, 2000. (Published in Korean.)

Korean American Clergywomen's community. The Korean American Clergywomen's community has been influential in shaping my call and vision for ministry. The community has helped me understand where I stand in The United Methodist Church and in the world.

Involvement in the Korean Language Conference

Since my early days in ministry I have been involved in the life of the general church of The United Methodist Church. I was one of the first two Korean American women elected to the General Conference, in 1996. The 1996 General Conference, held in Denver, Colorado, was a pivotal time for the Korean American community, because it was then that a petition came before the body to create a Korean language/missionary conference. This petition became a dividing issue. The Korean American Clergywomen's Association had voted to oppose the petition and formed a five-person task force, but not without differing opinions. As one of the task-force members, I wrote a statement that was widely circulated among the 1996 General Conference delegates and participants. In it I stated that we did not believe the language conference would be helpful for future generations. As clergywomen, we sought to inspire each other to stand for what we believed was right. We believed that the creation of a language conference would further isolate and marginalize Korean Americans from "mainstream" United Methodism. I believed that we were already marginalized from the center; so, I asked myself, "Why should be push ourselves even further from the center?" We were also concerned about how those ministers who chose not to join the language conference would experience further disadvantages. I remember consulting with

Bishop James Thomas, who advocated for the abolishment of the African American central conference (an organization similar to a language conference) and helped the formation of The United Methodist Church in 1968. I still clearly remember Bishop Thomas sharing about the harm done to African American churches by their central conference. He said African American churches were further separated from the rest of the church due to the central conference. We did not want this to happen to Korean American United Methodist churches.

The Korean Missionary Conference petition was rejected at the 1996 General Conference, and the aftermath was not pretty. The issue continued to divide the Korean community into two opposing groups. The conflict and pain between and among Korean churches reached its peak between 1996 and 2000. The division was not just between the clergywomen and clergymen, but it was among the clergywomen themselves too, which was one of the saddest things that happened in our short history.

During this time of conflict, however, Korean American clergywomen continued to grow in their leadership as individuals and as a group. While prejudice persisted against Korean American clergywomen, many were emerging as leaders slowly, but surely, in their respective annual conferences and across The United Methodist Church connection. A couple of clergywomen even took an office at the general church level; I was one of them.

My Ministry: Church as a Place of Empowerment

Ironically, the church has been a double-edged sword for me—a place of struggle and yet at the same time a place of empowerment. I have experienced discrimination and prejudice in the church. But, at the same time, the church has also provided me with opportunities for growth and leadership, especially in ministries of justice and peace. The United Methodist Church has nurtured me in the womb of radical hospitality, risk-taking mission, and prophetic and reconciling voice.

I have been blessed to serve in diverse ministry settings. I have worked at various church levels including the local church level, the district level, the annual conference level, and at the national and international levels of the general church. In all of these contexts, I have lived my passion for mission and ministry. In a way, I broke new ground as I joined with others in the march for an inclusive and diverse church. I was the first Korean clergywoman who became a senior executive at a general agency. I was also the first Korean clergywoman to become a district superintendent and then a director of connectional ministries. I was one of the first ethnic pastors in the Rocky Mountain Conference to receive a cross-cultural appointment. I have been at the forefront of the battle for an inclusive and diverse church in my annual conference. My cross-cultural experiences in Anglo churches has led me to develop cross-cultural training events for churches and pastors that have been held in our conference.

My days with the General Board of Global Ministries (GBGM) helped me develop a deeper appreciation for the global expression of Methodism. It was a tremendous opportunity to grow as a person as well as a church leader. Many of my learnings were formed while working with my missional colleagues at the GBGM, where my vision and passion for an inclusive and diverse church sought expression in the global church. In my service as deputy general secretary for the GBGM, my passion led me to work in the areas of peacemaking, ecumenical and interfaith dialogue, and global AIDS ministries, in which I am deeply involved to this day.

As a district superintendent I have worked with churches to accept and embrace racial-ethnic cross-cultural appointments. I helped my district implement the Hispanic plan of the denomination by creating a new Metro District Coordinator position for Hispanic/Latino Ministries. I also helped set the stage for emerging church worship in several of my district churches. My vision for an inclusive and diverse church goes beyond racial-ethnic and gender inclusion, as a strong advocate for the full inclusion of the LGBTQAI+ persons. As director of connectional ministries, I led the church to a clearer vision of making disciples of Jesus Christ and aligned our resources for that vision. I focused my energy on developing new churches. I lived out my commitments to revitalize existing congregations.

This vision also includes more participation by young generations. In my most recent ministry as superintendent of leadership development, I have been called to wake us up to a new generation that longs for the church to be more relevant. I have been a consistent voice for developing the leadership of younger generations. Consequently, I created an academy for newly ordained clergy. The purpose of this academy is to nurture young clergy for their lifelong transformational ministry.

Transforming My Marginality

Marginality is a theme that runs through my life and ministry. And yet, I have strived not to be paralyzed by it. My response to the context of marginality has been to transform, not conform. This process has taken a couple of forms.

First, I overcome my marginality through marginality.[6] When I meet people in marginal spaces my marginal identity gets transformed. When I hear a gay person sharing her experience of living on the margin, for example, I know I can meet her there. I feel empowered when my marginality meets others' marginality. My marginality is transformed into a vision for full inclusion of all humanity. My marginal racial and gender identity creates an intersection rather than division and exclusion. While the intersection of these margins can be debilitating, it allows me to redefine the meaning of the margin, making it a place of empowerment. It is transformative to experience the margin as a place of empowerment. Therefore, I don't necessarily try or want to move from the margin to the center.

The fact that the margin can be normative took me a whole lifetime to realize. It is okay to be on the margin. I am OK on the margin. Professor Jung Young Lee explains it this way:

> We have a tendency to think that marginalized people are saved or rescued by people at the center because they dominate our society—since they have marginalized the poor, the weak, and the different. As long as the ideology of people at the center is normative, everyone wants to be at the center. Genuine liberation comes only when the norm shifts from the center to the margin.[7]

---

6 Jung Young Lee, *Marginality*, 151.
7 Jung Young Lee, *Marginality*, 149-50.

So, my work is to help move the norm from the center to the marginal space where I am. It is my ministry to help create an inclusive church and inclusive community.

I love the way that the Canaanite woman speaks to Jesus about marginal space, saying, "Even the dogs eat the crumbs that fall from their masters' table" (Matthew 15:27, NRSV). She is a foreign woman. She is an outsider. And she speaks to Jesus out of her marginal space. She calls Jesus to draw his vision bigger and embrace those who are on the margin. She is saying he is no longer a savior called only to the Jews but also one called to the Gentiles. The Canaanite woman is now included in Jesus's new vision of the kin'dom of God. I feel as if I am this Canaanite woman, inviting others to come to a new understanding of who we are and what we are called to do. My work has been to draw our circle wider and wider, to include women, gays and lesbians, Koreans and Hispanics, old and young. I strive to transform my experience of marginality by joining in the shared struggle of all humanity—especially of the people on the margin. I join in a collective vision of new life. I want to keep the vision of an inclusive church and the vision of an inclusive humanity alive.

Finally, I attempt to transform the marginality by continuing to cross bridges. I crossed the bridge of immigration to come to this country. I crossed the bridge of cultural expectations to ordained ministry as a woman. Throughout my life and ministry, I have not only crossed many bridges into a new and unfolding future but have strived to build bridges of hope for others. There are always more bridges to cross and more bridges to build. When I fight against sexism, the barrier of racism appears. And the mighty winds of a rapidly changing world always rush in.

As I write this essay, The United Methodist Church is crossing a bridge over troubled water—possibly facing the creation of a new expression of Methodism. A tide for inclusiveness insists that we—The United Methodist Church—respond. Our challenge is that "the bridges that we are crossing are not fixed, but moving targets that lead us to multiple directions, not just one."[8] When I cross a bridge that might lead to a certain destination, I often find out that I have arrived at a place different from what I expected. Where I stand, I preach. I teach. I train. I pray. I seek to lead with vision for an inclusive church. As a Korean American clergywoman, I have learned the hard way that God's table must be open to everyone, and therefore I work to lead the church into a truly inclusive and multicultural community. I continue to seek God's *shalom* by embracing the global vision of The United Methodist Church.

My story is in the present perfect tense: "has been." It started in the past and is continuing in the present. Women and people on the margins are not only the past of the church, we are the present and future. My story is not yet complete. It continues. It is a part of a larger story of women—a community of women who came before me and the community of women who will come after me and continue to dream. My story is born out of the story of my mother, my grandmother, and my great-grandmother. And my story will be part of the story that my daughter's generation will live out. I face down

---

8   Diana Butler Bass, *Christianity for the Rest of Us: How the Neighborhood Church Is Transforming the Faith* (San Francisco: Harper SanFrancisco, 2006).

today's fears, so that tomorrow's women might offer their ministry with courage.[9]

I am a Korean American clergywoman who lives on the margin. Nevertheless, I lead.

---

9   See Alice Walker, *In Search of Our Mothers' Gardens: Womanist Prose* (San Diego: Harcourt Brace Jovanovich, 1983), 235–37.

4

With Wisdom, Wit, and Resistance
Women in Church and Society in Germany

Rev. Rosemarie Wenner, Retired Bishop, Germany,
The United Methodist Church

There is no longer Jew or Greek, there is no longer slave or
free, there is no longer male and female; for all of you are
one in Christ Jesus.

—Galatians 3:28 (NRSV)

Introduction

In 2003 the Woman's Division of The United Methodist
Church in Germany published a book on the history and
the stories of women in The United Methodist Church. Its
title is *With Wisdom, Wit, and Resistivity.*[1] Wisdom, wit, and
resistivity—each of these character traits is needed in the
work for equal rights and the full inclusion of women in society and the church. Since the church is always embedded
and, in part, influenced by the society, I will start with brief

---

1   *Mit Weisheit, Witz und Widerstand, Die Geschichte(n) von Frauen
    in der Evangelisch-methodistischen Kirche*, Herausgegeben vom
    Frauenwerk der Evangelisch-methodistischen Kirche (Stuttgart:
    Medienwerk der Evangelisch-methodistischen Kirche, 2003).

remarks about women's history in Germany, before I come to the church.

Women's Rights in Germany

At the elections to the National Assembly of 1919, women for the first time were allowed to vote. Thirty-seven of the total of 423 deputies in the newly elected parliament of the so-called Weimar Republic were women. Amongst them was Marie Juchacz (1879–1956), a member of the Social Democratic Party and founder of a Worker's Welfare Association, which still exists today. Marie Juchacz was the first female voice to be heard in a German Parliament. She said:

> It is the first time in Germany that a woman has been able to speak freely on an equal basis in parliament to the people. I would like to note here, and I believe that I speak for many, that we German women are not bound to thank this government in the traditional sense. What this government has done is only natural. It has given women what they had hitherto wrongfully been denied.[2]

The right to vote was an important step, but it did not mean full inclusion in public life. After World War II women won the fight to include equal rights in the Constitution of the Federal Republic of Germany (the so-called West Germany). Article 3 reads: "Men and women shall have equal rights." Despite this achievement, it was not until 1969 that married women were allowed to have a job or open their own bank

---

2   https://www.bundesregierung.de/breg-en/search/marie-juchacz
    -the-first-woman-to-speak-in-parliament-1582438.

account without their husband's signature. In the German Democratic Republic, which existed from 1949 to 1990 and belonged to the Eastern Bloc during the Cold War, women formally had better conditions. They were not only allowed but even expected to work, and their decisions about birth control and abortion were in their hands. Nevertheless male superiority prevailed and even today, the struggle for equal rights continues in the now united country. When compared to men's wages, on average, women work as many as 77 days per year without pay, given the fact that they are not equally paid. And only recently have women dared to tell stories of sexual harassment and abuse as a part of the #MeToo movement.

Woman's Division: A Space for Engagement and Empowerment of Women in the Methodist Movement

In 1887 the Methodist Episcopal Church in Germany and Switzerland officially created a Woman's Foreign Missionaries Society. Women met in groups, called clubs or societies, in order to do needlework and other crafts to raise money, not only for female missionaries abroad but also for the theological education of the male candidates for ordained ministries and other needs in their conferences. In his report to the Central Conference in 1930, Bishop John Louis Nuelsen (1867-1946) requested the representation of women in the conferences in Europe:

> It is clear that one cannot expect women to take big efforts to raise money and afterwards men decide upon its use. I think it is of high importance to find a way to secure the joyful and enthusiastic work of

51

women and to grant them appropriate and fully satisfactory representation in the leadership.[3]

It took until 1968 when the Methodist Episcopal Church and the Evangelical United Brethren Church were united for the presidents of the Woman's Divisions of the annual conferences to become ex officio members of their conferences. At that time there were very few other women conference members. Despite those struggles the work in the women's societies bore fruit. Women broadened their perspectives through their involvement in foreign missions. They organized themselves and supported one another in their daily lives and in their struggles for inclusion.

Because of the political situation The United Methodist Church in Germany had to divide into two central conferences from 1970 to 1992; consequently the same was true for the Woman's Division. In the Central Conference of the Federal Republic of Germany, Maria Wunderlich (1910–1980) served as president of the Woman's Division starting in 1968. She challenged women to take responsibility for church and society and to engage in discussions and initiatives related to equal rights and self-determination of women. Maria Wunderlich was also the editor of a magazine for women. As early as 1975 she wrote of the importance of Feminist Theology. Although there was resistance in the Central Conference, it was agreed that the Woman's Division was allowed to work with its own budget and to decide how to spend the money raised by the women. Half of the income was spent for foreign mission, one-fourth for the education of women in order to develop female leaders

---

3 *Mit Weisheit, Witz und Widerstand*, page 248, translated by Rosemarie Wenner.

in The UMC in Germany, and one-fourth for the work of the Woman's Division itself.

In the German Democratic Republic (GDR) 90% of the women were employed. On one hand it sounds like a step toward equality, but on the other hand for many women it meant having several full-time jobs at one time. Housekeeping tasks as well as taking care of childcare were still seen as women's work. In this situation it took special efforts to organize programs for women in local churches and at the conference level, and as a result new forms of being together were created, that is, retreats for women and children. In the German Democratic Republic sending missionaries abroad or inviting them to visit churches was nearly impossible. Nevertheless women in these churches wanted to support women in other parts of the world, so contacts with sisters in other Communist countries became important.

The contacts between the two women's organizations in greater Germany never stopped. Women from West Germany traveled to the East and many letters were written back and forth. This was especially true in the broader Methodist network. The Federation of Methodist and Uniting Church Women helped women stay connected. In 1989 the Woman's Division in the GDR together with the sister organization from the Federal Republic of Germany hosted the European Area Seminar of the World Federation in Potsdam, GDR. In one of the worship services everybody received a candle. A woman from Great Britain said: "I will keep this candle as a reminder to pray for the unification of Germany. I will light it after Germany is one country again!" Nobody believed that a few months later the peaceful revolution—inspired by candles and prayers—led to the moment when the gates of the Berlin Wall were opened and people danced with one another in the city of Berlin.

The work for inclusion continued. The Woman's Division fought for a quota related to the composition of the Executive of the Central Conference. Starting in 1992 each annual conference had to elect at least one female delegate. This is how I became a member of the Executive of the Central Conference in 1992. Consequently I became known in all the conferences and was later elected as the first female bishop of The United Methodist Church outside of the USA.

Empowerment of women is still needed today. But the work of the Woman's Division is not valued and recognized to the same extent that it was even in more recent years. Younger women have many responsibilities in their professional careers, family life, and the church, and many women are satisfied with the level of inclusiveness their foremothers achieved.

Female Clergy

The decision of the General Conference 1956 to grant full clergy rights to women had no immediate impact on the conferences in Germany. The 1950s were instead a time of restoration of an old way of living in families and churches. During World War II, women preached and led, because, often, men were not available. But as soon as peace was established and men came back, the old role allocation was reinstalled. The first woman to be ordained in one of the conferences in Germany was Hildegard Grams (1920-2007) after she was trained in the Theological Seminary of the Methodist Church in Frankfurt, Main. She was the only woman of the fifty-six students. After finishing her studies, she was sent as a missionary to India. In 1959 Hildegard Grams was ordained in Berlin. Bishop Friedrich Wunderlich (1896–1990) explained in the church magazine that the Church in India had requested that ordination. Hildegard Grams never became a clergy member in her home conference in Germany or in a conference in India. She founded and led a school for girls in Batala, North India, where she lived until 2001.

Theological training for women was a strong emphasis of the Woman's Division. After training, women served as catechists or youth workers in local churches. In the conference journals they were named "Assistants in Local Churches." The assistants had a form of recognition through their conferences, but if they were granted conference membership, they counted as lay members. One of these "assistants" became the first ordained female clergy in The United Methodist Church in the Federal Republic of Germany. Christel Pohl (subsequent to her marriage, she became Christel Grüneke) was educated in a training center for female catechists and served as local church assistant in North Germany. After a few years she entered the ordination process and was ordained in 1969 in the Germany North-West Annual Conference. Summarizing her experiences as "the first," Christel Grüneke said:

> Of course several people simply saw me as a "token woman," because I was the first clergywoman in The United Methodist Church in Germany. Even less familiar was the service of a female pastor to most of the funeral directors or in Roman Catholic hospitals. But with humor, serenity, and my certificate I was able to manage all those situations. Skeptics in my own church realized that being a female pastor did not mean performing a dream job in order to

become emancipated but [was] a step of obedience as a disciple of Jesus.[4]

I was the third woman to be ordained in The United Methodist Church in the Federal Republic in Germany and the second in my home conference, the Germany South West Annual Conference. My elder colleague Rev. Gertrud Michelmann, who was ordained in 1977, supported me in many ways. However, in all of the ministries, I had to overcome resistance. When I was asked, "Why are you a pastor when the New Testament does not support female leadership?" I answered simply by telling the story of how I realized that I was called to become a pastor. Several people in the local church later admitted, "I just could not imagine that a woman would serve as preacher and leader in the church." One year after I took a new appointment in a three-point charge near Heidelberg, my fiancé and I decided to get married. I waited until the district superintendent visited the church in order to inform the congregation that I would soon be a spouse. When I announced the wedding, a woman who was very active in various ministries said, "I do not know whether I am willing to accept that change." The district superintendent said, "This was just a point of information! Any pastor has the right to marry!"

In part the resistance of some church members was grounded in the fact that several Protestant Churches in Germany did not allow their clergywomen to marry until the mid-1970s. To combine full-time ministry in the church with one's responsibilities as a spouse and possibly as a mother was seen by congregations as an unreasonable demand. They

---

4 *Mit Weisheit, Witz und Widerstand*, page 235, translated by Rosemarie Wenner.

were used to a male pastor and his spouse. The spouse was supposed to be a volunteer co-worker in the local church. Today clergywomen are no longer an exception. Girls and women are part of a church with female role models for all kinds of ministries and leadership positions.

Back in the 1990s the following conversation took place. A female pastor told her family at the lunch table that a young man of their local church wanted to become a candidate for ordained ministry. At that time I was the district superintendent in the area and two female pastors served in this two-point charge. The pastor's five-year-old daughter said, "What? How can a man become a pastor?"

She was not the only one thinking that the pastor's work was mainly for women. Several people assumed ordained ministry soon would become a mainly female profession. That did not happen. Today 22% of those who are actively serving as ordained elders in the three annual conferences in Germany are women. We still have a few congregations where women clergy are not welcome, and consequently the appointment of a female pastor would not be accepted. In most places, however, female pastors are welcomed.

Inequality plays a bigger role, however, as soon as we speak of leadership positions: There is only one female district superintendent out of nine in the Germany Central Conference. The fact that I was the episcopal leader of the Germany Central Conference for a twelve-year tenure did not increase the number of women in committees and leadership roles. (I even got the impression that unconsciously many people in the church were assuming that women are well enough represented with a female bishop.) It is also fair to say that some clergywomen do not make themselves available for tasks with high visibility for increased public recognition. They see particularly clergy leadership as male-dominated, and they are afraid that it will be too stressful and time consuming, leaving no time for their families or themselves.

However, inclusion of women at all levels in the life of the church is more than a justice issue. It is about becoming who we are called to be—a diverse community that values, shares, and uses the fullness of God's gifts and graces in order to build up the body of Christ for its ministry to all the world. We proclaim in our Social Principles:

> We call upon women and men alike to share power and control, to learn to give freely and to receive freely, to be complete and to respect the wholeness of others. We seek for every individual opportunities and freedom to love and be loved, to seek and receive justice, and to practice ethical self-determination. We understand our gender diversity to be a gift from God, intended to add to the rich variety of human experience and perspective; and we guard against attitudes and traditions that would use this good gift to leave members of one sex more vulnerable in relationships than members of another.[5]

Only if we live together as a community that mirrors "There is no longer Jew or Greek, there is no longer slave or free, there is no longer male and female; for all of you are one in Christ Jesus" (Galatians 3:28, NRSV) will we gain credibility in our Western society, where more and more people identify themselves with "no religion."

---

5 *The Book of Discipline of The United Methodist Church, 2016* (Nashville: United Methodist Publishing House, 2016), ¶ 161 F, S. 112.

Conclusion

The journey continues. We have not achieved gender justice. Even more problematic, we ignore the fact that women are still not fully included in the life of The United Methodist Church in Germany. Many women say, "We are satisfied with the reality. We are part of the church and we are part of the civil society. We have equal rights. And we are far better off than women in most other countries of the world." The latter is true. Yet it is also true that there is more work to do even in Germany. We have to become a church where we all together grow in awareness of the beauty of God's amazing grace at work in all human beings and in the whole creation.

One of my favorite stories in the Bible is the story of how Christianity came to Europe (Acts 16:6-15). After a journey with a lot of "trial and error," Paul had the vision to set out for Europe. Then he and Timothy took the next boat and landed in Samothrace. The first place for them to preach the gospel was Philippi. There was no crowd listening, just a few women. Women did not count in order to achieve the number of ten worshippers that were needed for an appropriate service in a synagogue. Paul preached to the women. Among them was Lydia, owner of a purple business. Lydia became a follower of Christ and was baptized. She immediately understood that she was called to the ministry. She invited Paul to stay in her household, which then became the worshipping space for the first congregation in Europe. Paul was hesitant, but Lydia urged him to recognize her faith and also to receive her gifts. She acted with wisdom, wit, and resistivity. Lydia prevailed upon Paul and Timothy. Church history in Europe started with a woman as leader in her house church. This is a legacy for the European church. Wisdom, wit, resistivity, and resilience are needed to continue the journey in building communities of Christ's disciples that are a foretaste for the heavenly banquet. All are welcome. Women, men, bisexual people, transsexual people, asexual people, children, youth, elderly people. All are affirmed with their gifts. All are needed in order to transform the Church and the world. All are called to bear witness to God's love, which knows no boundaries or restrictions.

5

Leading from the Heart

Rev. Dr. Ouida Lee, DMin, Retired Elder, North Texas
Annual Conference, The United Methodist Church

For surely I know the plans I have for you, says the LORD,
plans for your welfare and not for harm, to give you a future
with hope.

—Jeremiah 29:11 (NRSV)

The Gospel of John is my favorite book of the Bible, and a cornerstone of this book is foundational to the way I offer leadership as a servant of the church.

I give you a new commandment, that you love one another. Just as I have loved you, you also should love one another. By this everyone will know that you are my disciples, if you have love for one another. (John 13:34-35, NRSV)

In a world so filled with brokenness, as a leader I am challenged to live a life dedicated to loving others. It is also important to know that this leadership comes from a call to ministry and is characterized by servanthood. Leadership in ministry is servant leadership. And when I speak of "servant," I am speaking as one who knows her God and the concern that God has for the people God loves, which is all of us. A servant leader is one who has been empowered by God to know that nothing is impossible with and through God. A servant leader is a faithful follower who believes and teaches that without faith it is impossible to please God, a servant who knows that God knows the plans that God has for you—a future full of hope to encourage and not harm you. A servant leader is one whose faith is confirmed by the love of Jesus Christ, yet one who has been tried and tested in every way, one who is willing to let go of ego and all of the trappings that can tempt one to believe that feelings of superiority have a place in the work of the ministry of Jesus Christ.

But servant leadership is not about weakness. It is about strength—the strength to stand up, speak truth to power, and act with assurance that only comes from being a child made in God's image. Upon reflection, as I began to write this chapter a memory flashed in my mind about my mother. Mother was a maid, a servant, for a prominent family in our community, and though she prepared meals for the family, she was told to use the outside toilet. However, whenever I visited mother at work, she would say to me, "Use the bathroom in the house." She never allowed me to use the outside toilet. I did not understand it then, and it wasn't until during my seminary training when I was introduced to Womanist Theology that it became clear. Mother, who had only an elementary school education, understood the sting of being treated as second-class, and she knew that she wanted better for her children. It was her love for her family that made her stand and block the door of the bathroom, if the lady of the house came home unexpectedly while I was there. Taking the lessons my mother taught me, I have come to realize that servant leadership as practiced in the church, which is predominantly Eurocentric, is misunderstood. It is not about being subpar or subservient, but it is about obeying God and helping bring in God's reign. So I add my voice to those of Dr. Jacquelyn Grant, Bishop Teresa Snorton (CME), Dr. Renita J. Weems, and Dr. Katie G. Cannon as they teach African American women in pastoral leadership how to stand against the evils of racism, sexism, and classism.

Leading from the heart is easy once one gains the respect and cooperation of the congregation, even if that might take a long time. This is where leaders have to lean and depend on God's grace. Previously I served a two-point charge in a small, rural town. As a servant leader in these small congregations, it was easy to host a meeting, share my vision, and invite the participation of the congregational leaders. As a leader, I shared a vision, one that I extended to the congregations as well, inviting them into a preferred future of what we, together, hoped to achieve. It was our hope, our road map, not just my hope and what I wanted to achieve. For these churches the vision described the intent to protect our children from the social ills of the community. When we were clear on the vision and had buy-in from the congregational leaders, we embarked on our journey, equipped with God's grace going before us.

Leadership in ministry is focused not only on the church but also on the identified needs of the community. My heart was sincerely touched as I observed a community in decline, houses in need of repairs, and children playing in the streets. As a concerned pastor and congregation with a vision for the small congregation, we set goals and recruited people within our community to begin building teams.

A good leader is aware that goals cannot be accomplished by any one individual alone but require teamwork, and it is the leader's job to create the conditions in which teamwork can flourish. John Maxwell, author of *The 17 Essential Qualities of a Team Player: Becoming the Kind of Person Every Team Wants*, says team players must be adaptable, teachable, creative, emotionally secure, and service minded. Team players must be collaborative, dependable, competent, enthusiastic, and mission conscious. I was particularly impressed by these words about team members: "They do whatever is necessary to accomplish the mission" (Maxwell, 94). Those are the kinds of people we all like to work with.

Communication is key and critical to successful servant leadership. One must have the ability to explain things clearly, so that everyone understands the goals and how each task is to be carried out. Unlike large corporate organizations, the church does not always have the income to hire staff; therefore, much of the responsibility for communication rests on the pastor. Further, it is important for the pastor to lead with transparency, listen to the feedback of the members, and keep them fully informed about the process and the procedures that will take place. Within the context of small congregations, as well as larger ones, motivation is very important. The leader has to inspire the congregation in order to build supportive teams, and it is important to know what motivates the individual member of the team in order to gain a better buy-in and be able to mentor, where necessary, those who have a real interest in the particular project. In the case of our community, we wanted the children to have a safe playground, out of the general flow of traffic. Safety of children alone provided enough impetus for people to get involved, and with community support, the church built a playground.

Despite successes such as these, women who are pastoral leaders are often challenged in the African American Church. There are questions about what the Bible says regarding women in the pulpit and having authority in the church. And even within denominations where women are ordained by their judicatories, these concerns are raised by men and many women who have come from various more conservative denominations. Because the role of strong African American women is often questioned, and their leadership is challenged by other strong women within the congregation, it is necessary to keep focused on the mission of the church and the importance of grace, rather than get embroiled in the mire of congregation politics if at all possible.

In these difficult situations, leadership, especially leadership from the heart, requires that women have the ability to be creative and stay focused on the Great Commission, "Therefore go and make disciples of all nations, baptizing them in the name of the Father and of the Son and of the Holy Spirit" (Matthew 28:19, CEB). Dr. Katie Cannon reminds us in *Katie's Canon: Womanism and the Soul of the Black Community*, "In essence, the Bible is the highest source of authority for most Black women" (Cannon, 56). As God-fearing women, they maintain that Black life is more than a defensive reaction to oppressive circumstances of anguish and desperation. Rather, Black life is the rich, colorful creativity that emerges and reemerges in the quest for human dignity, and Jesus provides the necessary soul for liberation.

Leadership of Black women from the biblical perspective is not limited to simply preaching, even for the edification of the congregation, but includes chipping away at oppressive structures. We cannot afford to take the back seats or to repeat what others may perceive as a "good word"—one that will make us comfortable even in our harsh realities. The Bible gives us exemplars of men and women who, like us, have faced incredible odds and succeeded.

Servant leadership takes shape by creatively developing workshops and seminars that focus on the issues that plague the community and prevent us from being safe. This can spark other creative persons to think of nontraditional strategies to solve problems and then evaluate their work and listen to feedback. Receiving positive feedback helps people build confidence that can propel teams to do greater work.

Leaders know that both the success and failure of the team's work are their responsibility. A good leader is aware that it is okay to delegate work to others, but that does not absolve the leader's responsibility. As much as it is a good thing to be in touch with and available to those to whom the work has been delegated, it is always a good thing to acknowledge your mistakes. Being transparent with your limitations can model for the team that when mistakes are made, and there will be mistakes and missteps, honesty is best and can serve to make the team stronger in the long run.

Commitment is a vital part of leadership, especially in ministry. A leader's determination is especially necessary for those who have given up on life and those who are continuously battling racism in the public square. The leader, within the context of community, should have as a personal goal to empower people to face the challenges of a world that has gone wild, only seeks material gains, and desires instant gratification and good feelings without challenging the status quo realities. Leaders should offer their churches a commitment to train and empower others who will do the kind of ministry that frees the bodies and souls of the people. But of course, commitment also requires following through, perseverance, prioritization, and a work ethic that is in touch with the realities of our society. This means speaking more than a prophetic word from the Bible. It means teaching people survival skills. Leadership is the commitment to tell stories, as Bishop Vashti McKenzie shares in *Journey to the Well*: "Stories have the power to teach, train, inspire, motivate, encourage, and change minds, habits, and perceptions" (McKenzie, 2).

Leadership is to know that you are called to lead even in times of opposition. It was a Tuesday night and I was to be appointed as senior pastor in a cross-cultural role. I was to arrive at the church at approximately 6 p.m. and be introduced to congregation at 6:30. I was told to remain in the car and I would be invited in. I sat in the car wondering what was taking so long. Finally at 9:30, I was invited to meet the Staff Parish Relations Committee. I did not have a good feeling about what was taking place.

Later, on my first Sunday at the church, I visually noticed that several members of the SPRC did not come to worship, and they never did return to the church. How does one lead through storms in one's life? With prayer, faith, and determination. The church was theologically conservative, and I would be the first African American and female to head the congregation. And as usual, I did my homework and learned that the church was located in a racially transitioning community. I studied the demographics and saw there was a growing number of single female-headed households. As a person of prayer it became my goal to organize a prayer team to meet weekly on Saturdays. I had experienced the difference that prayer could make in the life of a congregation. We later also organized a weekly Thursday night online prayer call with the intent of reaching more of the congregation with prayer. Typically, the administrative council met on

Sundays following worship, and during the preceding week various committees met in preparation. One week, I was particularly invited to the finance team. During the discussion, the team wanted me to know that the church did not have any money. I said that we should ask each family to contribute $1,000 toward the treasury. I was told that I had not been there long enough to ask the congregation for that kind of commitment. The meeting concluded with the decision that the committee would announce to the church council that we had no money.

On Sunday following worship, the council met. When the finance team was asked to report, they said: "We have no money." Everyone looked at me. I shared that I had asked the team to ask each family to give one thousand dollars. Then I said, "Since I would never ask you to do anything that I was not willing to do. . . . Although you all have not paid me my first check, I did get the final one from my previous church." I wrote the check for $1,000 and laid it on the table and sat and looked at each leader of the council. We received $17,000 at the table that day. There are times when leaders have to "put up or shut up."

John 2:13-15 says that Jesus had to confront the people about the way they treated their brothers and sisters who were making their annual pilgrimage to Jerusalem. The money changers were in the Temple making a profit from the sale of animals for sacrifice. Jesus confronted them. It is a known strategy among churches who wish to refuse an ethnic minority pastor to withdraw their money until another pastor is sent. It was clear in my mind that giving money is a heart matter. If members of the congregation were withholding their money until they got their way, I wanted to respond with courage and lead by example.

As it happened many members moved their membership within the first six months of my arrival. But also during that time forty new members had united with our congregation. The church was growing. In an attempt to get to know the entire membership better, I hosted meetings at the parsonage. During those times, people remarked on the growth. They wanted to grow but not this fast. Yes, members left but new ones came—people who reflected the face of the community. We were growing . . . more diverse. But even if the membership declines, a leader does not sit and commiserate over the loss; good leaders lead the congregation in facing the crises inside the church and outside in the community. Our church established an evangelism team, made plans, set goals, developed brochures, and gave invitation cards to all members. A team of us made home visits and wrote letters to first-time guests. We hosted prayer walks in the community. We hosted Bible studies in local restaurants, giving added visibility to our church.

As a new leader in the community, it was my goal to interact with the community, finding the needs so that the church might attempt to fill them. Therefore, it was my recommendation to adopt the elementary school that was near the church campus. We hosted a report card review program with the children of the school and provided pizza parties for those who attended. Through meeting with the school principal, we learned of the plight of some of the students who had no meals on weekends. The men's ministry adopted a project to provide food that could be taken home by the children in their backpacks. We learned the statistics about teen pregnancy in the schools and a team of educators, business people, and nurses established a purity abstinence program that was held at the church for three months on Sundays. The youth of our congregation, along with their friends, attended the class, and at the graduation ceremony, each teen received a commitment ring.

As leaders in the community, we addressed another need that we identified in our school, and that was to provide supplies for children returning to school. As the team met, another opportunity emerged, this one for the adults in our community. Since we had a parish nurse in our community, we decided to include health screenings for adults in cooperation with Methodist Health System. This is an annual program and includes activities for children while parents are screened.

With a vision of open doors, open hearts, and open minds, we adopted a safe alternative to Halloween with a Trunk-R-Treat on the parking lot and extended invitations to all the elementary schools. Games and fun-filled activities filled the lot as the children enjoyed their safe play time. And when the weather was cold, we brought the activities inside, where there were treats in every classroom. Each family was given invitations to worship on Sunday and they received a free meal, as we celebrated Bring a Friend Sundays.

Caring for physical needs such as health screenings is important and fun activities like the Trunk-R-Treats are entertaining, but people also need spiritual care and nurture. So to address these needs, the church hosted an annual "O Give Thanks Revival." During the fall of each year the church held a three-night revival leading into the season of Thanksgiving. And in the beginning of each year, we hosted a prayer breakfast and invited members of our community to share with us.

Leadership does not neglect the church's financial needs. When the air conditioner needed replacing, we established a "Beat the Heat Campaign" and raised the funds to pay for it. And in order to reach our annual budget, the finance team recommended special fundraisers. One fundraiser was the "Tree of Life Campaign." This program invited church members to give extra money the entire year to supplement the budget. One of the most beautiful fundraisers was the "Debutantes for Christ Pageant," which did raise funds but was also meant as a motivator for the youth ministry.

As important as the local church is, it is not the only locus of ministry, and leaders should be open to serving in voluntary roles outside of the church. Through my connection with Perkins School of Theology, I served as a mentor to students and the church became a training congregation for student interns. Their assistance facilitated the work of our youth and children's ministries.

As I close this chapter about pastoral leadership and review my work, I am thankful, but simultaneously I see additional ways that I could have possibly made more of a difference. There are mountains and valleys associated with leadership, and I, like any leader, have experienced difficulties and disappointments, but above all, I am thankful that God allows me to lead from my heart.

PART 2

WOMEN
ARE
THE CHURCH

Jesus Says: "I Am the Vine"

Rev. Motoe Yamada Foor, Senior Pastor,
Sacramento Japanese United Methodist Church,
Sacramento, California

I am the vine, you are the branches.
Those who abide in me and I in them bear much fruit,
because apart from me you can do nothing.

—John 15:5 (NRSV)

"I am the vine, you are the branches."

I was born and raised in Tokyo, Japan. My father was a Zen Buddhist monk, although when I was growing up, he was not working as a monk and was an editor at a publishing company. My parents divorced when I was ten years old and their divorce led me to some soul searching. After the principal of my elementary school told us that the children in Africa were dying, I started to cry. I realized that I was not the only child who was suffering; and maybe, there was something I could do for them. I started to work on children's rights, and later women's rights. In the process, I fell in love with Mahatma Gandhi and decided to devote myself to social justice and human rights. Since I wanted to work for the United Nations or an international human rights organization in the future,

I needed to learn about different religions and have a better understanding of people in the world. My first Christian worship service that I attended was at Mukyokai (no church denomination)—a gathering at someone's house. Although I do not remember the sermon, "my heart was strangely warmed," and I felt that my sins and burdens from my parents' divorce were lifted up and forgiven. Yet, I was too stubborn to admit that I might have been touched by God, so I ignored the experience. (In Japan since World War II, people generally consider that religion is bad and is for weak-minded people.)

In 1995, I moved to Toledo, Ohio, to attend a university to learn English and study international relations. I did not speak English and I didn't know anyone in the United States, so every experience was new. It was a struggle to be an immigrant and woman of color in the Midwest. After a few years, I adjusted to the college life and decided that I wanted to learn about the Bible, because I was in a "Christian" country. I met Rev. Denise Baker of the Toledo campus ministry, and she is the one who led me to Christ. I was also amazed by the Christian community and how much they seemed to care about me. I immediately felt a calling to ministry; however, I could not decide right away, so I went to get a master's degree at Michigan State University. Meanwhile, I was elected as a steering committee member of the United Methodist Student Movement, which opened new opportunities to meet more Christians and learn about Jesus. It was also a great leadership opportunity for college students, especially women, and I am so proud to see that, by God's purpose, many of the friends from that group are now denominational leaders at different levels, such as pastors, church lay leaders, conference staff, and general board staff. I carry their friendship, shared experiences, and our journey in faith with me every day. Jesus is the vine and we are his branches!

During that time, one of the significant conferences I attended was the International Youth Leadership Conference for the World Methodist Council in London. There were two women (myself and another) who were the finalists to represent North America for the World Methodist Council. After ten rounds of voting, we were tied, and the tension was high between the two groups, each supporting their own candidate. Ms. Brittany Isaac was the other candidate, someone I knew and highly respected. After much prayer, I decided to step down as a candidate. Whatever we do, we are to glorify God's name. Brittany did excellent work representing North America, and later she became a pastor and now serves as a district superintendent. If you believe that someone else is capable and if you let the other person take the opportunity, God has another door waiting for you. That's exactly what happened to me when God led me to be a United Methodist representative to CESCM (the Council for Ecumenical Student Christian Ministry) and the North American Regional Committee for the World Student Christian Federation.

There were many young people's movements at that time, and it was my honor to be co-chair of the US Conference of the World Council of Churches Young Adult Task Force. I met many wonderful Christian leaders throughout the year. As young women, we promised each other that we would receive our education and get the credentials we needed, so that people cannot tell us that they could not find qualified young people and/or women. One of these women who made that promise is Ms. Kathryn Lohre, who became the twenty-sixth president of the National Council of Churches. Currently she travels the world as the Executive for Ecumenical and Inter-Religious Relations of the Evangelical Lutheran Church in America. She is also the mother of four children! Anything is possible with God!

Later, I became one of the four United Methodist members on the World Council of Churches (WCC) Central Committee (2006–2013) and vicechair of the Ecumenical Networks Committee for the National Council of Churches. Christians around the world are working together for justice and peace! I also learned the beauty of worshipping Jesus in different styles through my experiences with these organizations. At the WCC General Assembly in Porto Allegre, Brazil, thousands gathered under a tent for worship, and it was as though God was whispering when everyone said the Lord's prayer in their own tradition/language. ("Bless our God, O peoples, let the sound of his praise be heard," Psalm 66:8, NRSV.) During the assembly, I was one of the two young people to organize global youth (18- to 30-year-olds) to start the WCC commission on youth. When we branches connect to the vine, Jesus, many wonderful things can happen!

"Abide in Me."

Through the ecumenical experience, I was able to meet diverse groups of pastors, which later helped me discern my calling for ministry. When I was in the Midwest, I only knew a few women pastors, none of whom were a racial-ethnic minority. At my first meeting with a pastor to discuss pursuing ordination, he discouraged me from going into ministry. I later found out that many other women had similar experiences with this same pastor. Even though I believed that God was calling me, it was difficult to understand how God would call someone like me. I was a young Asian, a woman, a new Christian, and a person who did not speak English well. But God had a plan for me! ("For surely I know the plans I have for you, says the LORD, plans for your welfare and not for harm, to give you a future with hope," Jeremiah 29:11, NRSV.) Do not let anyone tell you that you were not called to ministry, or tell you who you are, because God uses every one of us! Abide in Jesus!

Although I started to attend seminary (Graduate Theological Union/Pacific School of Religions), I wanted to serve in an organization such as the WCC but not in a local church. But when I did my first internship with Buena Vista United Methodist Church in Alameda, California, I fell in love with the people and the local church. The church had multiple community organizing projects, and one of my first projects was to start an afterschool program for low-income and struggling youth. Here I witnessed the pain of immigrants' children yet also the hope they inspired in me. One of these youth later became a youth director, and I am so proud of him. Spreading Christ's love to others and seeing people's lives transformed are some of the many blessings of serving in a local church. Abide in Jesus!

As we have all seen, some people like to complain about their situation and yet do nothing about it. When I was going through the ordination process, social media was not available; communication was more limited, and not everyone received the same information about ordination requirements. As a result, some of us were held back a year because some mentors did not know about a required retreat, so I started a seminary group so that we could exchange critical information and no one would be left behind. Abide in Jesus so we can do more!

Moving to California and being a part of Japanese American churches, I was surrounded by "Abiding in Jesus" stories about Japanese Americans' internment camp experiences. During World War II, President Franklin Roosevelt signed Executive Order 9066, which called for the relocation of Japanese people in the United States. Most of the 120,000 Japanese forced to relocate were American citizens. People told me how heartbreaking it was to leave their homes with only two suitcases and how horrible the conditions were in the barracks. It was frightening because they did not know what would happen to them next.

I have heard these stories many times, especially when I meet with families to prepare for their loved one's funeral. Being sent to an internment camp is almost always mentioned along with the significant impact it had on the person's life. Yet the amazing thing is that in the midst of the struggle and pain, people found hope in Christ. I am so inspired by their faith and perseverance. Mixed with the sadness, horror, and uncertainty, many Japanese Americans survived the internment camps and returned with faith, hope, and a steadfast determination to stand up and speak up in order to prevent this from ever happening again. Abide in Jesus!

Their own experience at the hands of government has made Japanese Americans also stand up against the racial profiling of Muslims, especially after the 9/11/2001 attack on the United States, because they believe that no one should be treated how they were treated. As many Japanese American churches are becoming more pan-Asian, I hope we will continue to remember this history, so we will not repeat it.

Abiding in Jesus even though we are discouraged is important! I worked as an associate pastor under Rev. Mariellen Sawada Yoshino's leadership at Wesley United Methodist Church in San Jose, California. Although we are called by God and do everything we can to make disciples, ministry can be difficult. For example, when I was facilitating a weekly young adult Bible study, there were nights that no one showed up. But we need to keep trying and trusting that God will plant the seeds. You never know how the seeds will flourish or where they will grow. Right before one Easter, I met Ms. Karen Yokota, whose parents are committed church members. As I was inviting her to my young adult Bible study, in my head, I was telling myself: "There is no way she will come to the Bible study. She lives an hour away, and she would not drive after her busy work to join this Bible study." However, Jesus has done amazing things. She did start coming to the Bible study. She also went on the young adult mission trip, and later she heard her calling from God for ordained ministry. Now she is serving as an ordained pastor and will be serving in a large church this coming July. We never know how God is using us to reach out to others. So, keep inviting people to Christ! Abide in Jesus!

"Bear much fruit."

In The United Methodist Church, the number of racial-ethnic clergywomen is increasing. However, at times, it is difficult to do ministry, because some people have never met someone like me. For example, whenever I go to a public place such as a hospital, I always wear my collar and a nametag, because without them, most people would never guess that I am a pastor. Therefore, it was my joy to form the Asian American and Pacific Islander Clergywomen's Association during the Racial-Ethnic Clergywomen Consultation in 2008. The idea for the association began when I saw that the consultation schedule did not include Asian Americans or Pacific Islanders. The Japanese clergywomen invited all clergywomen who did not have a group to belong to. During the lunch, we discussed why there was no association for Asian American and Pacific Islander clergywomen. With the help of Rev. Dr. HiRho Park, we decided to form one and met the next morning to vote on the bylaws and elect officers. During the closing worship, one of the women bishops and our other racial-ethnic sisters blessed our new association (aapicumc. org). When we met at our first AAPIC biannual gathering, we found out that each one of us had been discouraged by family, pastor, friends, and/or churches from even going into ministry. Therefore, we created a peer coaching ministry to help young women who are considering going into the ministry. If you are discerning your call or in an ordination process and need help, please feel free to contact me.

The year 2009 was a significant year for me because I was ordained and appointed to Sacramento Japanese United Methodist Church, where I instantly fell in love with the church and the members. I felt that God made me for this church. I was also the first woman senior pastor appointed to this church and twenty years younger than any senior pastors they had previously had. When I started my appointment, the church was divided. "For just as the body is one and has many members, and all the members of the body, though many, are one body, so it is with Christ" (1 Corinthians 12:12, NRSV). I listened to all sides of the story and did my best to remain on Jesus's side. I loved the people and saw God in each of them. And God brought us together.

During my early years, we came up with a church vision—"Loving God, Serving Others, Transforming Lives." Ninety-six people joined the Lenten small group, and the church formed a mission committee to serve the community, including an ongoing partnership and meal program with two charter schools neighboring the church. Our mission outreach has grown and expanded in so many ways over the years, and people's lives are touched with the love of Jesus Christ. I want every person to know that they are loved by God and to also find a ministry which they feel they are made for by God!

My church has experienced me as a single woman, then a married woman, then being pregnant, and now a mother with two kids. Although I had more time when I was single, God provides differently for different chapters of our lives. With my own children, I was able to connect more with young families and see more of them at the church. We need to listen to God and how God wants to use our gifts, talents, and experience. You never know what is waiting for you!

In November 2015, a week after my birthday, my daughter was born. Ten days later my mother passed away. I was not able to be with her physically since she was in Japan, yet I felt God's grace that my mother passed as she was listening to one of her favorite songs, Cherry Blossom/Sakura, sung by me. What we learn from our mothers, we pass on to the next generation. We have tons of wonderful women in our history and we need to continue to carry on their strong, brave, and creative legacy. Also, we need to open more doors for the younger generations to come.

In the California-Nevada Annual Conference, we are blessed by many wonderful women leaders: Bishop Minerva G. Carcaño, the first Latina bishop in United Methodist Church history; effective district superintendents; many inspiring women clergy; and faithful lay women. Our conference has organized churches in groups or circuits, and I am a circuit leader of ten churches. I love working with my circuit pastors. I also coordinate the ministry of a mega circuit (three circuits in the greater Sacramento Area). There is beauty in working together in supporting one another and sharing resources. Our ten-church group of circuit pastors has had a joint Pentecost service at a local park and a Rise Against Hunger where we packed 20,000 meals. We hosted "Immigration Day," disciple-making (TeamWorks) workshops, a combined big youth event, and various other events together. Let's bear fruits in Jesus's name! Together we can identify the strength of each church and collaborate to make more disciples and to reach out to more people in our communities with the love of God and Jesus Christ.

From earliest times, the church has always been supported by women, and the current and future church cannot stand without women. If you are a lay member or a pastor, young or old, put your head high and proclaim the Good News. You are fearfully and wonderfully made, and there is something God wants you to do in your life! "I praise you, for I am fearfully and wonderfully made. Wonderful are your works; that I know very well" (Psalm 139:14, NRSV). I am currently participating in the Academy of New Church Starts and am very excited about new ways of doing ministry to reach out to more people!! Let us bear fruit in Jesus's name.

Last, as I study the scriptures, I increasingly realize that the meaning of my name Motoe—*moto* means "the origin of everything" and *e* means "branch" in Japanese—is "I am the vine, you are the branches" (John 15:5, NRSV). I am thankful for my family, who support me in my journey. I am blessed to know wonderful church people and inspiring friends, colleagues, and mentors. Most of all, I give all glory to Jesus Christ, our Lord and Savior. As the scripture says, we need to abide in Jesus to bear much fruit. So let us continue to make disciples of Jesus Christ for the transformation of the world.

Empowered Women
Transforming, Enabling, Discipling

Rev. Connie Semy P. Mella, ThD, Associate Dean for Academic Affairs, Union Theological Seminary, Cavite, Philippines

Zipporah gave birth to a son, and Moses named him Gershom, saying, "I have become a foreigner in a foreign land.

Exodus 2:22

Who are women leaders? What are their roles? Their roles are life-giving. Women leaders transform, enable, and disciple. For thousands of years under patriarchy, women have been relegated to the margins and considered the weaker sex. In this chapter, by "patriarchy," I mean the "legal, social and economic system of society that validates and enforces the domination of male heads of families over the dependent persons in the household. The dependents normally include the wife, dependent children, and slaves."[1] Under the DOSE (domination, oppression, subjugation, and exploitation)

---

1   Rosemary Radford Reuther, "The Religious Sacralization of Patriarchy" (undated paper).

system of patriarchy, women are put in the margins; and chauvinist thinking, defined by male superiority, becomes a prevailing notion and often denies the possibility of women's leadership. Patriarchy sets aside and then forgets the values of community, equality, mutuality, partnership, and wholeness for women and society more generally. Sadder still is the fact that, under patriarchy, even women are conditioned to accept their inferior status as the norm.

However, the Bible can give us clues how to address and overcome patriarchy. The Exodus story is held as one of the, if not the, most important events in the life and faith tradition of the Jewish people. Its impact far exceeds a one-time event for a single people but constitutes an ongoing experience in human history.[2] As Jews today remember the Exodus story, they reconstitute this memory, making it a moral imperative, a commitment, not just to recall, but to work for liberation. While Moses remains the most recognized figure in this momentous story, we cannot discount the role women played. The roles of Zipporah, Jochebed, Shiphrah, Puah, Bithiah, and Miriam, in particular, are worth pursuing.

Women Leaders Preserve Lives[3]

A consistent theme of Exodus is that women save the life of Moses. In the first chapter, readers witness the fearlessness of the two midwives Shiphrah and Puah, who go against the orders of Pharaoh to kill all Hebrew baby boys. "When you act as midwives to the Hebrew women, and see them on the birthstool, if it is a boy, kill him; but if it is a girl, she

---

2   www.myjewishlearning.com/article/the-exodus-effect/ (retrieved: June 26, 2019).

3   See Exodus 2:21-22; 4:24-25; 18:1-6.

shall live" (Ex. 1:16, NRSV). The midwives disobey Pharaoh's orders because they fear God (or perhaps they fear their God more), "and because the midwives feared God, [God] gave them families" (Ex. 1:21, NRSV). God rewarded them.

But it is not only the midwives who protect the life of Moses. There is Moses's mother, Jochebed, who is creative and ingenious enough to look for ways to protect him for three months. There is Miriam, Moses's sister, who courageously watches her baby brother, thereby ensuring he survives, and then speaks up when the Egyptian princess asks for a woman to serve as the baby's nurse. Then, there is Bithiah, the Egyptian princess, who adopts Moses and introduces him to Pharaoh's household, ensuring his future. Through their actions all these women give and preserve life.

Zipporah

Later when Moses flees into the wilderness, he encounters Zipporah and her sisters tending the sheep of their father—Jethro the Midianite priest. Zipporah is one of Jethro's seven daughters and the one who eventually weds Moses. "Zipporah" is a Midianite name that means "a little bird," "a sparrow." The root of this word is the Arabic verb that signifies "to chirp."[4] After a time, she and Moses have two sons, Gershom and Eliezer. While we often overlook Zipporah's role in Exodus 4:24-26, it is clear that she protects Moses as they travel on their way to Egypt. According to Exodus 4:24, when they stop on their journey, "the LORD met him [Moses] and tried to kill him." In response, Zipporah takes a flint, cuts off her son's foreskin, and then touches Moses's "feet" with it ("feet" being

---

4   Herbert Lockyer, *All the Women of the Bible* (Grand Rapids, MI: Zondervan Academic, 1988), 168.

a euphemism for sexual organs).[5] Zipporah says, "Truly you are a bridegroom of blood to me . . . a bridegroom of blood by circumcision." Consequently, Moses escapes unharmed. Exactly what this passage means is open for debate, but clearly Zipporah's action is vital for Moses's survival.

Also noteworthy is the similarity in the sound of the names, "Zipporah" and "Shiphrah," the midwife.[6] As these stories were originally told rather than read, the sound conveyed by the words is important as the story was intended for the ear rather than for the eye. Given the similarity of these names, the listener would naturally associate them and understand both women are attempting to do the same thing—protect Moses so that he can fulfill his destiny and lead the people into the Promised Land. Not only does Zipporah give life as a mother, her actions preserve the life of Moses, his family, and ultimately the Hebrew people.

Miriam

Miriam[7] was a prophetess, a leader, and yes, a sister. She is remembered primarily as Moses's sister, yet she was so much more; she was a leader. Edith Deen, in her book *All of the Women in the Bible*, says that Miriam was the first woman in the Bible whose interest was national and whose mission was patriotic. Perhaps this is overstated, but Miriam led the

5   Exodus 4:24-26 has been variously translated, highlighting the fact that scholars disagree about the meaning of Zipporah's action. But she is decisive and seems to be aware of what needs to be done.

6   Herbert Lockyer, *All the Women of the Bible* (Grand Rapids, MI: Zondervan Academic, 1988), 168.

7   See: Ex. 15:20-21; Num. 12:1-15; 20:1; 26:59; Deut. 24:9; Micah 6:4).

women of Israel in what might be considered the oldest of all national anthems, "Sing unto the Lord," as they danced and celebrated the escape from four centuries of bondage in Egypt.

Miriam is first introduced as a little girl in Exodus 2:4,7. She stood by as her mother, Jochebed, made baby Moses an ark, put Moses inside, and launched him into the water. We can presume that even at a young age, Miriam exhibited bravery, wit, and wisdom. As an adult Miriam was a prophetess (Ex. 15:20). As such, she was not only a spokesperson of Yahweh but also a person of wisdom whose words would have been a powerful compass that guided her people. The Talmud tells us that even as a child, God spoke to Miriam: when Pharaoh threatened to kill all male Hebrew children, Amram,[8] Miriam's father, not wanting to see any of his sons killed, left his wife, as did all the other Israelite men. As a result, Miriam chastised him, saying, "Your decree is worse than Pharaoh's. He decreed against the boys, but you will end the lives of the girls as well."[9] Accordingly, Amram listened to his daughter and remarried Jochebed. Their reunion resulted in the birth of Moses, who, as we know, became an agent of the liberation for the Hebrew people.

The book of Numbers also tells us that God spoke to Miriam. Scripture gives us a complex picture. On one hand, Miriam is described as courageous and straightforward, yet when she and Aaron ask, "Has the LORD spoken only through Moses?" (Num. 12:2, NRSV), Miriam is punished with leprosy and banned from camp for seven days. However, the Bible

---

8   Amram was the husband of Jochebed and the father of Aaron, Moses, and Miriam, as stated in Numbers 26:59.

9   Jill Hammer, *The Jewish Book of Days: A Companion for all Seasons* (Philadelphia: The Jewish Publication Society, 2006), 393.

also notes that the people of Israel do not resume their journey until she is reconciled with them.

What makes her so important that the tribes will not travel unless Miriam goes with them? Jewish tradition says that a miraculous well followed Miriam in the wilderness and lodged in front of the *mishkan*,[10] a place of healing and comfort, where trees and sweet-smelling fruits grew.[11] The Babylonian Talmud (Shabbat 35a) tells us the well can be found "to this day" in the waters of the Sea of Galilee,[12] and some people place a cup of fresh water on the Seder table in honor of Miriam.[13]

In her popular book *The Jewish Book of Days*, author Jill Hammer has this to say about Miriam:

> Even in the days when her life is bitter from slavery, Miriam knows one day she will stand at the shore of the Sea of Reeds and feel that she is free, and she will dance. This dream makes her a pillar of fire, guiding us through the waters to freedom. Miriam is like the sun, leading the people through the dark waters of the sea into the bright wilderness. It is striking that as a girl, Miriam dreams of the Sea of Reeds and sees the water part.

---

10 Aramaic word meaning "an abode of God," "a dwelling place," or "a tabernacle."

11 From Song of Songs Rabbah 4:14; Midrash Tanhuma, Be-shallah 21-22, as quoted by Jill Hammer in the book *The Jewish Book of Days: A Companion for All Seasons* (Philadelphia: The Jewish Publication Society, 2006), 226.

12 Jill Hammer, *The Jewish Book of Days*, 226.

13 During the celebration of the Passover Seder at Union Theological Seminary, Cavite, Philippines, in 2014, Miriam's cup of fresh water was among the elements in the Seder table.

Perhaps this is why, at the time of the Exodus, Miriam brings musical instruments with her, so that the women will have timbrels to play when they celebrate their freedom. In "Kislev"[14] as we approach Hannukah, season of renewed sun and renewed freedom, we remember Miriam's dream.[15]

Through the acts of Miriam, the people's experience is transformed from suffering to healing and celebration. As women continue to lead, they have capacity to transform the Church and our experience of the Christian life. Women leaders do influence the life of the local church, the community, even the worldwide connection of the Church, so we can fulfill our destiny to live fully as the people of God.

Women Leaders Transform

At one of the national assemblies of the United Methodist Women Society of Christian Service in the Philippines, I was tasked to reflect on the topic "Empowered Women in Jesus Christ: Transforming, Enabling, Discipling." This theme is replete with challenges that I want to discuss here as well. Like the women of the Exodus story, women lead by being transforming agents.

Transformation is both a challenge and a calling. According to the Webster's thesaurus, the word "transform" is a verb which means "alter, change, or metamorphose." It means to

---

14 Kislev is one of the twelve months of the Hebrew year; it falls during November-December, with Hanukkah or the celebration of lights as an important holiday.

15 Jill Hammer, *The Jewish Book of Days: A Companion for all Seasons* (CreateSpace Independent Publishing Platform, 2018) 103.

change the shape, appearance, or condition of. The word "metamorphose" is usually associated with the process of becoming of a butterfly—from a crawling worm to a silent cocoon to a colorful being that can freely and beautifully fly from one place to another, one flower to another.

For women transformation can be a process of self-actualization: confronting one's fears, then allowing oneself to morph into embracing the true value of her worth. Women need to fully recognize and take hold of their gifts, potentials, and possibilities. Even when the patriarchy that surrounds them says they are worthless or second-class students, citizens, workers, leaders. Likewise, women are called to encourage other women to do the same, because none are free until all are free.[16] Then like butterflies, we can all fly. By understanding the depth and scope of our possible contributions, women will not only alter or transform their own situation of marginalization but also help others to create and sustain a more just and humane world.

One of the Filipino Methodist women leaders who helped in the transformation of Philippine society is Asuncion A. Perez (1895-1967). She served as the first woman member of the Cabinet of the Republic of the Philippines. She was a self-supporting student who worked her way through college by serving as Assistant Matron of the Hugh Wilson Hall Dormitory for Girls. She became a social worker for the Red Cross in 1924 and held such positions as Executive Secretary of the Associated Charities of Manila and the Red Cross. Perez then served as administrator of Social Welfare from 1948 to 1953; she was one of the original board of trustees of the

---

16 A paraphrase of Emma Lazarus's famous line, "Until we are all free, we are none of us free."

Philippine Rural Reconstruction Movement and founder of the Children's Garden of the Philippines. In September 1948, President Elpidio Quirino elevated her to the position of a cabinet member, making her the first and only woman to hold the office at the time. She served under four presidents: Manual L. Quezon, Sergio Osmena Sr., Manuel Roxas, and Elpidio Quirino.[17] She died on September 12, 1967, but her work is immortalized through an institution named after her, the Asuncion Perez Memorial Center Incorporated. The Center is a social arm of The United Methodist Church committed to the work of empowerment, integrity, social holiness, and human dignity.

Women Leaders Enable Others to Flourish

Women have a unique capacity to nurture and enable. One way women demonstrate this is through their inherent gift to give life. Many life-changing experiences as well as success stories have been attributed to the living-giving influence of women. When we talk about our Lord Jesus Christ and remember his birth, don't we also remember his mother, Mary? Who could forget the great influence of Susanna Wesley, whose strong faith and deep love guided her children, particularly John and Charles? Abraham Lincoln is well-remembered in history as the US President who signed the Emancipation Proclamation, which put an end to slavery. When interviewed and asked what enabled him to make a difference, he simply said that his guidance came from the words of his mother, "Abe, be good."

---

17 Phebe Crismo, "The Trailblazers: Filipino Methodist Women Who Did It First," in *The Filipino Methodist Magazine* (January-March 2018, Vol. 2, No. 1), 6.

Yes, some women are life givers—mothers—but we can do so much more to inspire and bring life. One of the Filipino Methodist women who made and is continually making a difference in the lives of many by enabling them to access education is Dr. Priscilla Viuya. Dr. Priscy, as she is fondly called, is the first Filipino Methodist woman president of a state university, the Tarlac State University from 2006 to 2016. "The first thing she did when she became president was to invite the janitors, guards, and secretaries to lunch, [and through this invitation] many [came] face to face with the university president for the first time."[18] She offered scholarships for working and struggling students. She served as director of the General Board of Higher Education and Ministry for eight years. She was an active member of Tarlac City United Methodist Church and is currently president of Ecumenical Christian College in Tarlac City. She is also the founding president of the Philippine Association of Methodist Schools, Colleges, Universities, and Seminaries (PAMSCUS).

Women Leaders Disciple

To be a disciple is to be a follower of Jesus. It means to do what Jesus is doing—to be engaged in the ministries of preaching, teaching, and healing. A disciple follows Jesus, who commands us to love God with all our hearts, minds, and souls and to love our neighbors as we love ourselves.

I want to lift up the ministry of teaching, which is central to the mission and ministry of the Church. For 152 years, the General Board of Higher Education and Ministry of The United Methodist Church has existed to facilitate the

---

18 Crismo, "The Trailblazers," 9.

education of students worldwide and strengthen educational institutions related to the Church. We have more than one thousand schools, colleges, universities, and seminaries all over the world. Filipino women educators continue to take part in this noble task. One who blazed the trail is the Rev. Dr. Elizabeth S. Tapia, the first Filipino Professor at Bossey Ecumenical Institute of The World Council of Churches.

Dr. Eliz, or "Ate Eliz" as she is fondly called by many, is a "pastor, teacher, and theologian who is passionate about mission, theological education, cross-cultural studies, and leadership development."[19] She served as the first woman Academic Dean of Union Theological Seminary in Cavite, Philippines, and at Christian Conference of Asia, and she served as a technical consultant whose work paved the way for the creation of the CCA's Women Desk. In 2002-2005, she served as professor of missiology at the Bossey Ecumenical Institute of the World Council of Churches in Switzerland—the first Filipina and Asian woman to serve as full-time professor there. She served and is continually serving in many other educational institutions, such as Harris Memorial College and John Wesley Theological Seminary in Tuguegarao, Philippines. Dr. Eliz is passionate in discipling people to be followers of Jesus Christ for the transformation of the world.

Women leaders indeed transform, enable, and disciple. They have the heart to persevere and the courage to face the challenges. Their hope springs eternal and their faith shines through. Even in the midst of uncertainty, they continue to hold fast to their calling. They have proven that, as agents of life, they can give birth to new possibilities and help people of faith find refreshment and renewal. There

---

19 Crismo, "The Trailblazers," 9.

may be contradictions and barriers along their way; yet, with their faith in God, like the women of Exodus, women leaders can turn stumbling blocks into stepping stones, barriers into bridges, hardships into inspiration. No matter what, women will continue to lead!

PART 3

WOMEN **WILL BE** THE CHURCH

Serving the Church in a Postcolonial World

*Rev. Alka Lyall, Pastor, Broadway United
Methodist Church, Chicago, Illinois*

I've said these things to you so that you will have peace in me.
In the world you have distress. But be encouraged! I have
conquered the world.

—John 16:33 (CEB)

It's a girl," I am sure they were told when I was born! I was
my parents' first-born child, in a country (India) where a girl-
child was not welcomed with the same enthusiasm and joy
as a boy-child was. They had two more girls before a son was
born to them, but all four of us were given the same privileges, the same nurturing, and similar freedoms.

Faith was an important part of our family, so church
played an integral role in my life. I am who I am because
of my parents and because of the church I grew up in. My
mother made many sacrifices for us. My father served in the
military and was often stationed away from home, but Mom
never traveled with him, so that their children could have a
stable childhood, a steady home. She took us to church and
Sunday school as often as she could. I cherish all those experiences. Even though I did not appreciate the fact that I could

not partake in Communion until my confirmation, I enjoyed the process of learning and growing in faith.

I am grateful for all that the Church has taught and given me. I have been blessed by this same Church that has also challenged me to my core. The Church has loved me and yet has caused immense pain. It has grounded me and has caused instability in my life. Through all of these experiences, the Church has given me a community where I can question, learn, and even be vulnerable. Church is my family, and I love my church family, with all its kinks and quirks. I recognize that it is made of imperfect people, like me, and that we all desire to bring God's kin-dom on earth. We are working toward it, as best as we can with our own interpretations of what that means.

Over the years I have had many amazing colleagues and friends who have guided and mentored me. In the next few pages, I will share with you some of the lessons that I have learned from them and as a woman of color in ministry. The experiences have made me a better person and a better pastor. I continue to unlearn the things that do not serve us anymore and learn from my experiences every day.

Love the People

The most important advice one of my mentors gave me as I was going to my first appointment was to love the people. The suggestion was to refrain from changing anything in my first year of appointment, but to learn about the people and to love them for who they are. My mentor explained that, once the people learn that you genuinely love them, they will be willing to make any necessary changes and journey with you.

My first appointment was in a rural community. The population was less than one thousand and the only people of color in the community were my family and me. I was following a pastor who was very well loved. Several months into my being there, I was copied on an email. The email was sent from the former pastor to a member of the church, whom I will call Mike. The former pastor refused to officiate at Mike's wedding, because he was no longer the pastor of the church. That is how I learned that Mike was planning to get married. I was hurt and felt rejected. "Did I fail as a pastor?" I thought, "Did I not love them enough?" After days of prayer and discernment, and remembering the words of my mentor, I invited Mike for a meeting. I told him that while his email caused me pain, I wanted him to get married in his church. We invited the former pastor to assist me in officiating. Mike had a beautiful wedding in his church.

My relationship with Mike developed over the years. He frequently reminded me that he did not need a female pastor. A few years later, however, when I was assigned to a different church, Mike was not happy. I received that as his acceptance of my ministry at his church. I was reminded of my mentor's words, "Love the people."

Keep an Open Mind

Having grown up in a country that was colonized, I had received what I call today a Westernized Christianity, and I viewed the gospel through the eyes of missionaries. I want to be clear. I am grateful for the missionaries that went to different parts of the world to share the gospel of Jesus's love. But, in that process, what we ended up receiving was their version of faith. I learned that the only way to God was through Jesus. I learned that anything that was not about Jesus was not about God. Consequently, a lot of Indian culture was labeled as "not Christian" and therefore "pagan." Yoga and meditation were foreign ideas to me until I came to the United States, not because I was not aware of them but because they had been labeled as "Hindu" practices. Today, both these practices are popular around the world, and I am proud to claim them as "spiritual" practices that originated in India, and therefore have more of a cultural connection than a religious affiliation.

Over time I have evolved and so have my faith and my understanding of God and church. I had learned that God was love, and that Jesus was the only way to God. While I still believe that God is love and that my way to God is through Jesus, I now believe that other people can have their own ways to God and that is OK!

I had learned that the Bible was the inerrant word of God, not to be questioned. I struggled with that idea for years. Now I believe that the Bible, authored by humans, gives us an understanding of who God is, but it is not the exhaustive expression of God.

I grew up with the teaching that we could only receive Holy Communion after Confirmation, because young children are unable to understand the significance of the sacrament. After many years in ministry and seminary education, I now realize that no one completely understands the mystery of the sacrament, so I no longer exclude children from the feast that is meant for the whole family.

When I came to the United States in 1996 to go to seminary, I had what I call a simple faith. I knew that God had created the whole world and that God loved me. I had with me my King James Bible with the words of Jesus printed in red. In seminary, my KJV Bible was replaced by the New Revised Standard Version, with the apocrypha, and eventually I began using the Common English Bible. I still have those Bibles. Every so often I use them to compare translations. But I learned that the red-letter sayings of Jesus are really someone else's memories.

I started to find new things in the Bible and started to question some passages and stories. I realized there are two creation stories in the Bible and that they are not the same. I began to wonder, "If God is love, then how are some people loved by God more than others?" I now believe that God loves everyone regardless of any labels or boxes that we create.

Over the years I have learned that sometimes the Bible contradicts itself and can easily be used to harm people, especially when scripture is taken out of its context. I continue to read the Bible with an open mind, wrestle with its stories, and find ways to understand its message for our current reality.

I am grateful for the teachers, colleagues, and friends with whom I can discuss my doubts. I am grateful to them for not judging me but helping me understand and experience a God who could not be contained in a book or boxed into any one interpretation or description. I am grateful that, today, I can see the Bible differently. I can believe it but also question it.

This willingness to read the Bible with an open mind can sometimes put one at odds with our own people. I am part of a culture and community that is proud of their "strong faith" in what can be only a colonized version of God. The space is difficult to navigate when you are one of the few who are willing to free our God from Westernized constraints and look at the gospel message with your own interpretation and reason. Sometimes that journey is lonely. I am not even sure if my family in India understands my interpretation of God's love for all people. And I understand that. I am rooted in the same culture. So, this is not easy for me either. I have much to learn, and I continue to try to unlearn the oppressive theology that has been our narrative for so long, and relearn what it means to be a true witness of the gospel and a follower of Jesus Christ.

I am also grateful for my current appointment, where I can extend God's welcome to all people, just as God desires.

In God's Time!

Throughout my life there have been times when I felt I was being treated unfairly; but over the years I have come to realize that things happen, not in my time, but in God's time. While I was never treated differently by my family because of gender, the world around me constantly reminded me that I was of a "lesser" gender. While I was growing up, the Methodist Church in India, the church that nurtured me, gave women opportunities to serve the church as laity, including becoming a deaconess, but it was not ready for women in ordained ministry. As a young woman in India, believing that becoming a deaconess was the only way for me to serve God, and being encouraged by an episcopal leader, I started the process. But it was not God's plan.

Then, in the late 1980s, while I served on the executive committee of the World Methodist Council, I was invited to attend seminary in the United States, again by a denominational leader, but it was not God's plan. I took from those two experiences that God was telling me that my pull toward ministry was my idea only, so I gave up, got a bachelor's degree in teaching, and started working at a mission school. Life started to become somewhat normal with marriage and a child. Years later, through a series of complicated circumstances, another opportunity presented itself. In 1996, after much prayerful discernment and persistent coercion from faithful friends, I registered as an international student at Garrett Evangelical Theological Seminary.

Finally, it was God's time.

Things started to fall in place. I could write a whole book about my seminary experience—about God showing up through friends and strangers who became friends. It will suffice to say here that the journey was not simple or easy, but it was blessed and God was faithful. I was following the path that God had opened for me, and those experiences strengthened my faith in God's faithfulness. Looking back, I see how everything worked out, but in God's time.

In early 1997, we started attending a church that became my home church in the United States. For the first time in my life, I met women who were in pastoral ministry, and the call to be in ordained ministry started to become clear. The pull that I had felt on my heart for many years began to take shape. I began the process for ordination. After graduating in the year 2000, I was appointed to my first assignment.

I am still impatient with God. I am frequently angry at God for not working on my timeline, but deep down I know that I need to wait for God's time.

Don't Take Yourself Too Seriously

India, like many other developing countries, has been served by missionaries. I am grateful for them nurturing and mentoring me and many like me. I hold many of them in high respect, but the ones I remember and appreciate most are those who learned to speak Indian languages and communicated directly with us. They demonstrated that they were in India to be in ministry with us, not to minister to us. Learning from those experiences, I always make a conscious effort to be in ministry with the people and not to the people of the church or communities I serve.

English is my second language, so I know I pronounce many words differently. I am no longer embarrassed by that. I remind myself and others that my pronunciation is different, not wrong.

Hear Between the Lines

As children, we speak, think, and imagine in binary constructs. But our expressions, language, and perspectives change as we evolve and grow even as adults. Years ago, when talking about race, a parishioner whom I will call Judy told me that she did not see color in people. At that time, I appreciated her comment. I even agreed with her. "She was right," I thought, "if we stop looking at one another as people of different colors or races or as people from different countries, but saw everyone as equal, we would be able to live as one people." Now I understand that my agreement came from my own colonized thinking. I understand that although Judy did not mean any intentional harm, she spoke from a place of privilege. God created us all in God's image with different skin tones and colors. When we claim to not see color, we are denying the existence of those of different skin color. We are erasing a part of their being. Experiences like this have taught me to hear the message between the lines. I have not only learned to claim my brown skin but also begun to reclaim my culture that colonized Christianity had labeled as pagan.

Maintaining Status Quo

I know rules are important. I follow rules—well, most of them. They give us a framework to function from. They bring order in life. But rules that become a burden or deny a person's identity are troublesome for me. Rules that are enforced simply to maintain status quo put me on edge.

Growing up, one of the most difficult rules for me was the inability to partake in Holy Communion during "certain days" as a woman. In a country that still was male-dominated, this felt like an added burden on women, placed by the church. I never understood. What could be so unholy about the most beautiful and life-giving process of our bodies? Needless to say, I never stopped receiving the sacrament, and God has yet to smite me.

I believe that the most important lesson Jesus came to teach us was the message of love. Jesus said, "You must love the Lord your God with all your heart, with all your being, and with all your mind. This is the first and greatest commandment. And the second is like it: You must love your neighbor as you love yourself. All the Law and the Prophets depend on these two commands."[1] I believe that any rule or interpretation that causes us to live in unloving ways with God or with one another cannot be of God. God calls us to stand on the side of love, even if it means bending some rules, going against the flow, or interrupting the status quo.

---

1   Matthew 22:37-40, CEB.

I want to be clear on one thing. I am not an expert by any stretch of the imagination. It is much easier to maintain the status quo and go with the flow. So this is not easy for me. I mess up all the time. And it is most difficult when I feel I am on my own, but I try my best to keep my "eyes on Jesus, faith's pioneer and perfecter" and trust in the support of the "great cloud of witnesses" on whose shoulders I stand.[2]

These are some of the lessons I have learned while in ministry, but I am still learning to do the first thing my mentor taught me to do, "love the people." I am not always loving or welcoming. I fail to trust in God. I have not been able to keep an open mind. I can quickly become defensive and often reactive, rather than responsive. But I keep moving forward.

The color of my skin, my gender, and my age still stand in my way. I have been pushed behind for all of those reasons. But I refuse to be pushed down. I know the God who called me has promised to always stand by me.

I am still learning to stand up for myself. I have learned that if I do not speak for myself then someone else has the chance to speak on my behalf, and my silence can be counted as an affirmation of the dominant view, neither of which can always be in my favor or reflect my opinion. As a woman of color, I am very familiar with the sins of racism and oppression. There are so many divisions among us. White supremacy has prevailed because we have allowed our diversity to become our differences. The recent actions of our special called General Conference[3] are an example. Each action

---

2 Hebrews 12:1-2, CEB.

3 The called session of General Conference of The United Methodist Church took place February 23-26, 2019, in St. Louis, Missouri. The purpose was to act on a report from the Commission on a Way Forward, authorized to examine paragraphs in *The*

and position seems to claim that ours is the only interpretation of God and God's love. We have to find ways to honor one another as God's beloved children. We are all beautifully created in the image of God with our diversity and will one day return to the dust from which we were created.[4]

I am also aware that there are many women and persons in this world who are called by God but who find the Church universal keeps closing doors on them and telling them that they cannot be leaders in the church or teachers of the gospel. In India, during my "church workers" training in the 1980s, there were many women who were gifted preachers. They were called to be teachers of the gospel, but they never pursued ministry because they didn't think their call could be recognized by the Church. I am grateful that God sent people in my life who guided me, housed me, financed my education, mentored me, and gave constructive criticism to help me become who I am today.

I pray for the day when all my siblings—women, people of color, people who are gay, lesbian, trans, and queer—will be free to serve the church they love and preach the gospel that has been life-giving for them. I trust that God created this world, is still part of this world, and continues to recreate. I know that my job is only to do the will of God. I know that the God who formed me, redeemed me, and called me by my name[5] has also promised to be with me. With that confidence, I keep striving to do the work that God has called me to do.

Book of Discipline concerning human sexuality and to explore options to strengthen church unity.

4 Genesis 3:19, NRSV.
5 Isaiah 43:1, CEB.

Closets Are Meant for Clothes, Not Clergy

Bishop Karen P. Oliveto, Mountain Sky Episcopal Area, The United Methodist Church

---

Do your best to present yourself to God as one approved by him, a worker who has no need to be ashamed, rightly explaining the word of truth.

—2 Timothy 2:15 (NRSV)

The fiftieth anniversary of women's full ordination rights in the Methodist Church occurred in 2006. As much as it was a source of pride and strength to see a poster depicting early women leaders of our denomination who helped pave the path for this historic moment, it was also heartbreaking. So many of the women depicted on the posters broke ground in more ways than one, although parts of their history were kept closeted, by choice or design.

In order to write about the future of LGBTQAI+ ministry and The United Methodist Church, it is important to know our past. LGBTQAI+ persons have been, are, and will continue to be members, leaders, and clergy within The United Methodist Church. LGBTQAI+ people were a part of the Methodist movement from its very beginning: in 1732, when still a Holy Club at Oxford, John Wesley regularly visited in Bocardo

Prison a man named Thomas Blair, who had been convicted of sodomy. Wesley worked to get the charges dropped so Blair could be a free man. Wesley's commitment to Blair ought to be a foundational lesson to us: society's stigma and prejudices should not invade the church. LGBTQAI+ persons bear the image of God and the church should do everything in its power to ensure that LGBTQAI+ persons can live free and full lives.

It is important to note that the word "homosexual" is a relatively recent term. Various sexual orientations and gender identities have been recorded in many cultures throughout human history. Not all cultures viewed diverse sexual orientations and gender expressions negatively. The Polynesian Islands, for instance, note a third sex: mahu. Mahus have held a revered spiritual and social role in these cultures. Missionary culture, however, stigmatized this once-revered status in many Polynesian islands. Many Native American tribes understood that some people are a two-spirited third sex—berdaches—which also provided a unique spiritual role in the tribe. A contemporary understanding of homosexuality, however, is a late-nineteenth-century phenomenon. K. M. Kertbeny, in an effort to oppose German sodomy laws, first coined the word "homosexual" in 1869. However, it was not until the 1880s that the term became popular, "adapted by people who wanted to make sense of their own experiences, which were not adequately explained by labeling them unnatural or immoral."[1]

From England in the 1700s to the United States in the 1800s, LGBTQAI+ persons continued to play a role in the

---

1 Margaret Cruikshank, *The Gay and Lesbian Liberation Movement* (New York: Routledge, 1992), 5.

church. Many early women leaders, in particular, lived their lives coupled with other women. Two examples of this are Francis Willard and Anna Howard Shaw. Anna Howard Shaw broke through the stained glass ceiling and was ordained in the Methodist Protestant Church in 1880. A medical doctor as well as clergywoman, Shaw was known as a fiery orator and spent most of her ministry as a leader in the women's suffrage movement. From 1888 until 1906, Shaw worked very closely with Susan B. Anthony. Lucy Anthony, Susan B.'s niece, became Shaw's life companion and secretary, and Susan B. was hereafter referred to as "Aunt Susan" by Shaw.

In a reading of Shaw's autobiography, one cannot help noting the number of references to other—and in particular single—women. From her earliest memories through the sunset years of her life, Shaw's primary professional and personal relationships were with other women: Frances Willard and her companion Anna Gordon, Miss M. Carey Thomas (president of Bryn Mawr College) and her companion Miss Mary Garrett, Miss Hay and her companion Miss Sweet are a few of the many women Shaw names in her book.

In fact, Shaw's community of women was often subject to much media scrutiny. Her cottage on Cape Cod was often a resting place for leaders of "the Cause," (women's suffrage), and they spent their days out of doors, fishing, chopping wood, and tending the garden. Special fishing clothes were made, and the younger women wore knickers while older women wore bloomers under short skirts.

Their retreat was the subject of much conversation, and rumors circulated about their "care free and unconventional life."[2] When a reporter came to interview Shaw, everyone was careful to wear traditional clothing and to receive the reporter in a formal fashion. Yet the reporter allowed her imagination to run wild and illustrated her article with a drawing of Shaw fishing in knickers with a handkerchief around her head. She entitled the article "Shaw's Adamless Eden."

How uncommon was singleness for women—in particular, for women of Shaw's educational background and professional commitment? According to American historian Lillian Faderman, these nineteenth-century women leaders found their relationships with other women to be their primary relationships and their source of sustenance. Many of these women set up house together and appeared to have long-term monogamous relationships with each other. The term "Boston marriage" was used to describe such a relationship, usually found between women who were generally financially independent of men, either through inheritance or because of a career. They were usually feminists, often pioneers in a profession. They were also very involved in culture and in social betterment, and these female values, which they shared with one another, formed a strong basis for their life together.[3]

It is not known whether or not these relationships were sexual in nature. Many surmises have been made both positively and negatively, yet none conclusively. Traditional Victorian notions regarding sex and women would make it difficult for people of that era to imagine these relationships

---

2   Anna Howard Shaw, *The Story of a Pioneer* (1915; reprint, Canton, OH: Pinnacle Press, 2017), 267.

3   Lillian Faderman, *Odd Girls and Twilight Lovers: A History of Lesbian Life in Twentieth-Century America* (New York: Penguin, 1991), 100.

as including a sexual element. The Victorian woman was considered morally and sexually pure. It is clear, however, that such a relationship was a union between two individuals who committed themselves to one another and their relationship. These relationships were socially tolerated during this era, and stories and articles about "Boston marriage" arrangements were printed in magazines, most notably in women's magazines.

Frances Willard was a Methodist leader in the Temperance Movement and a friend of Anna Howard Shaw. She was considered the most popular Methodist of her era. In 1880, as the president of the Woman's Christian Temperance Union, she was invited to address General Conference—the first woman ever invited to address this body. This set off a firestorm of debate, which surprised her. She wrote in her autobiography: "In our simplicity, we thought it the most natural thing imaginable thus to bring the work we loved back to the church that had nurtured us and given us our inspiration. . . . One would have thought, however, that something revolutionary had been proposed."[4]

Eight years later, she was among the first five women elected by their annual conferences to be delegates to the 1888 General Conference (GC). This too, resulted in an uproar, with the debate regarding whether or not the women should be seated lasting one week. It would not be until 1900 that GC would approve women delegates, and the first ones were seated in 1904.

Her commitment to women's rights extended to ordination rights. In her book *Women in the Pulpit*, Willard noted:

---

4   See https://archive.org/details/glimpsesoffiftyy00will/page/614.

> I believe women should be authorized as ministers in the church of God . . . man has no greater natural or spiritual rights than a woman to serve at the altars of the church, as minister of the Gospel. . . . If women can organize missionary societies, temperance societies, and every kind of charitable organization . . . why not permit them to be ordained to preach the Gospel and administer the sacraments of the Church?[5]

Willard wrote in her autobiography a section on "Companionships," in which she discussed the many women in her life with whom she shared an attachment. She also wrote about the same-sex relationships of her day:

> The loves of women for each other grow more numerous each day, and I have pondered much why these things were. That so little should be said about them surprises me, for they are everywhere. Perhaps the "Maids of Llagnollen," (in Wales) afford the most conspicuous example; two women, young and fair, with money and position, who ran away together, refusing all offers to return, and spent their happy days in each other's calm companionship within the house they there proceeded to establish. . . . In these days, when any capable and careful woman can honorably earn her own support, there is no village that has not its examples of "two hearts in counsel," both of which are feminine.[6]

---

5   See https://archive.org/details/womaninpulpit02willgoog/page/n81.

6   Frances Elizabeth Willard, *Glimpses of Fifty Years: The Autobiography of an American Woman* (Chicago: Women's Christian Temperance Publication Association, 1889), 641–42.

For Willard, relationships between women are "beautiful and blessed,"[7] while relationships between men and women are not and cannot be until the goals of the temperance, labor, and women's movement have been incorporated into the society. Even the literature of the period reflected the fact that if women wanted to live independent lives, they must do so outside of the marriage relationship.

A twentieth-century Methodist leader, Georgia Harkness, was the first female full professor of theology at a Protestant seminary, Garrett Evangelical Seminary, as well as the first female professor to receive tenure at a seminary. Harkness is well known for accessible and practical theology that addressed the social concerns of her day, including ecumenism, war and peace, women's rights, racial equality, and, toward the end of her life, equality for gay and lesbian people.

Harkness was a key player in the movement for full ordination rights for women. She herself was ordained a local elder, which did not carry with it annual conference voting privileges. In 1924, more than thirty years before women in the Methodist Church would be approved for full ordination rights, she wrote an article refuting arguments against ordination for women. At the end of the article, she concludes: "If there are men enough in the ministry to do the work and do it well, we are willing to let them. But where are they? We wonder if the advancement of the Kingdom is not more important than the maintenance of an ancient prejudice."[8]

---

7   Willard, *Glimpses of Fifty Years*, 641–42.

8   Georgia Harkness, "The Ministry as a Vocation for Women," in *The Methodist Experience in America Sourcebook*, ed. Richey et al. (Nashville: Abingdon, 2000), 490.

In 1939 she wrote that "to close the door to any persons possessing spiritual and mental qualifications is, in effect, to say that sex is a more important factor in Christian vocation than character, spiritual insight or mental ability." Harkness played a key role not only in women's ordination rights, but also in ensuring that women were well-represented in leadership positions in the denomination in the years following.

For more than thirty years, Harkness lived with Verna Miller. The two were introduced to each other by their pastor in Chicago. The two moved to Berkeley when Harkness was hired by Pacific School of Religion, and then upon retirement the two resided in Claremont, California. In one of her books, the dedication page reads: "To Verna who shares my home and my life and to whom the book and its author owe much."

Why did I include the past when I was asked to write about the future? Because our future is connected to the past, to those lives who worked for justice within and beyond the church to insure that there was a place at the table for every child of God. Without knowing our past, especially the parts that are hidden or erased, it is hard to imagine the future.

I am often asked, "What's it like to be the first gay bishop?" I inform the person that in fact, I am not the first gay bishop. I am the first *openly* gay bishop. This often elicits gasps from others when I am in a group. While there is documentation that I am not the first gay bishop,[9] there are others who, due to the times they were living in or other commitments, could not be open. While effective leaders, the cost to them and

9   See the *Texas Monthly* article here for more information: https://www.texasmonthly.com/articles/the-double-life-of-finis-crutchfield/.

the church was that they had to have a part of their lives hidden so that they could live out their call from God and serve the church faithfully.

The United Methodist Church is at a breaking point as it debates if all who bear the image of God have a role in the church. The question negates the reality, as this essay has pointed out: LGBTQAI+ people always have been, are, and will continue to be a part of The UMC, or any other expression of it that may develop in the future.

Because other LGBTQAI+ church members will experience what I did: a call from God that was too strong for a rule to squelch. I had my call to ministry when I was eleven years old. My mother, making sure she honored the vows she took at my baptism, started me in Sunday school when I was three. Once I stepped into that musty church basement, I knew I had come home. I loved the Bible stories I learned. I loved the way the music we were taught helped me grow in faith. And I especially loved feeling God's love and grace envelop me whenever I entered that sacred space.

I thrived in church and couldn't wait to go back each Sunday. Children's choir was added to the weekly schedule, and then youth group, and I soon was spending as much time as I could at church. Finally, one day my music minister asked me what I wanted to be when I grew up. "An astronomer!" I told him. And then he asked a question that blew my world open: "Have you ever thought about being a minister?" I had never seen a woman pastor, so didn't even realize it was an option for me. But at that moment I felt God fill my heart (perhaps this is what John Wesley experienced when he felt his heart strangely warmed?) and I *knew* this was what God wanted of me.

The ministers of my local church mentored me from that time forward. They gave me books to read and more music to learn and put me in leadership positions. At sixteen I preached my first sermon and at eighteen was given the keys to the church as the pastor invited me (and any post-high school young people who had an inkling of a call from God) to be a student pastor. All these things confirmed for me what I was called to do with my life.

My pastors saw and affirmed my call. My home church affirmed my call. My District Committee on Ordained Ministry affirmed my call. My Board of Ordained Ministry affirmed my call. And then I went to seminary.

Seminary education frequently deconstructs one's life and faith. In the midst of that deconstruction, I listened to the stories of my LGBTQAI+ classmates and realized that their stories sounded a lot like mine. I recognized that for most of my life I had been in denial about my sexual orientation. I had always known I wasn't like other kids my age; I didn't always fit in, and I never, ever was interested in dating. I didn't have a name for my feelings until I was in seminary.

This sent me into a painful period as I continued to deny these feelings. On top of it all, God was distant and silent for the very first time in my life. At the end of my first year of seminary, I literally ran away, hopping on a Greyhound bus in Oakland, California, headed for Nova Scotia, Canada (which is about as far away as one can run and still remain on the North American continent). I cried for hundreds of miles, a tear-stained Bible on my lap. Finally, somewhere in Utah, my tears were spent. I finally was able to articulate to myself, for the very first time, "I am a lesbian." Instantly, I experienced the peace which passes all understanding. And, more important, God was powerfully present once again. I learned such an important lesson: God never leaves us. We leave God when we fail to claim who God creates us to be.

I spent the summer trying to fit all the pieces of my life together: what did this mean to me personally, professionally? My call was still strong. At that time, The United Methodist Church had not yet tightened down on the ordination of LGBTQAI+ clergy. I continued to pursue ordination and received deacon's orders in 1982. And then something I never imagined happened: I fell in love for the very first time. This love opened my heart further than I ever thought possible. I discovered a greater capacity for generosity and compassion. I learned about the sacredness of love and how it brings us even closer to God, who is Love. I was a better person and pastor because of love's lessons.

This created quite an internal debate as I approached elder's orders. In 1984, General Conference added the following words to the Book of Discipline: "since the practice of homosexuality is incompatible with Christian teaching, self-avowed practicing homosexuals are not to be accepted as candidates, ordained as ministers, or appointed to serve in the UMC." But I was already ordained a deacon and was serving faithfully under appointment. My annual meetings with the Board of Ordained Ministry continued to affirm my call as the fruits of my ministry were evident in my appointment. I continued to move forward as a candidate until that time when the church no longer wanted my gifts and grace in ministry.

It often was a lonely way to be in ministry. As with those early women leaders, keeping a part of one's life closeted takes energy, energy that could be used for ministry. But there were other lesbians in ministry—a whole underground network of women seeking to be faithful to God's call as they served in silence across the entire denomination. We constituted a safe community where we could be our full selves, sharing our stories and supporting one another as best we could.

Over time, closets began to shrink as LGBTQAI+ people gained rights in the secular world. Young people came out and refused to enter a closet of silence. I watched in awe of seminary students I taught as an adjunct professor of United Methodist studies. They had been raised their whole entire lives in a church that had become increasingly restrictive of LGBTQAI+ participation in the life and ministry of the church. Yet, our Wesleyan spirituality and theology had taken hold of them and wouldn't let them go, even when they came out. While some left for other, more affirming denominations (this included LGBTQAI+ and straight students, who could not serve in a church that didn't welcome everyone; I saw some of our brightest and best young pastors leave), many stayed. Why did they? Why do we stay? Because it is The United Methodist Church that taught us of God's love for us, nurtured and encouraged our call, and affirmed us as we grew into that call. There is no other denomination that has our unique, practical theology as we join personal piety and social holiness. This is our home.

So what does the future hold for LGBTQAI+ persons and ministry? The Spirit will find a way where there is no way. Even if greater restrictions are put in place regarding LGBTQAI+ persons, young children will be led by the hand to their Sunday school class and be delighted by the lessons found in that classroom. They will experience God's love for them and seek to grow in their discipleship as followers of Jesus. Some will hear a call to ministry even as they recognize their sexual orientation or gender identity. If the denomination has become more restrictive, they will find ways to serve, much like those who went before them did. Because you can't squelch the Spirit's call. Like those early women leaders, responding to God's call when the church tried to close its doors to their leadership, LGBTQAI+ people will continue to serve at every level of the church.

Native American Women in Leadership
A Circle of Voices

Rev. Anita Phillips, Retired Elder, Oklahoma Indian Missionary Conference, The United Methodist Church

---

Therefore, since we are surrounded by so great a cloud of witnesses, let us also lay aside every weight and the sin that clings so closely, and let us run with perseverance the race that is set before us.

Hebrews 12:1 (NRSV)

Through this chapter I am privileged to stand alongside my sister authors and share thoughts and reflections on women's leadership. And further, to address leadership from my perspective, that of a Native American clergywoman. In my essay, I have chosen four of my own memories of Native American women and girls, which provide a foundation for consideration of some of the contributions from our community toward effective church leadership in a multicultural world. I pray my sharing might contribute to the celebration of the hundredth anniversary of women's right to vote in the United States.

While I celebrate 100 years of voting rights as a woman in this country, it is important to note that I will not yet be able to celebrate 100 years of voting rights for all Native Americans until 2024. My essay thus celebrates both my identity as a woman and my identity as a *Native American* woman.

Books intended to share many perspectives toward a common focus most often utilize an organizational framework to offer a starting point for consideration of the content. Such is the case for *Nevertheless She Leads*. My sister authors and I share our stories from one of three headings: women from our respective communities *have been* the church, *are* the church, and *will be* the church.

Although our book is divided into these three sections, many of the authors can make a strong argument that our stories might fit under more than one or all three of these rubrics. This is the place from which I speak.

One of the key identifiers for the voices coming from this volume is that we speak from a *postcolonial global perspective*. This particular descriptor is crucial when listening to voices from the Indigenous Peoples of the world. Today, there are few, if any, tribes of people living a precolonial existence. While the remainder of the world claims a postcolonial perspective, it is important to understand that the majority of the world's Indigenous Peoples continue to experience life directly or indirectly impacted by the core tenets and/or vestiges of colonialism.

Childhood Memories of Grandma

I am a young child living with my grandmother in the rural hills of Cherokee County in northeastern Oklahoma. We heat and cook with wood. The smell of Grandma's house is delicious with that woody odor. We haul water from the river or draw it from the well. I watch my Grandma as she cares for her small home and cares for all of us who live here. We gather eggs, dig potatoes in our small garden, and collect wild onions along the creek bank. The watermelon patch is one of my favorite places as I witness the amazing transformation of a tiny blossom to a small green fist to a great rounded melon that tastes so good, mmm. . . .

There was an easy rhythm to life then. My uncle, one of Grandma's brothers, lived with us. Uncle Coleman was an important part of my life. I would learn later that maternal uncles were traditionally important in raising children within our culture. They helped with teaching and guidance. Uncle Coleman was a kind man.

Although I directly experienced the leadership of the women in my family, I later learned the Cherokee were one of many Indigenous Peoples who were matrilineal in our familial and social structure. Our women held important roles and their voices were respected.

We did not go to a Christian church, but Grandma had a Cherokee Bible that she read. It was printed completely in the Cherokee syllabary, which was created by Sequoyah, an early educational leader from our tribe. We also belonged to a Ceremonial Grounds where I learned we were part of the Long Hair Clan. As one of the seven sacred clans of the Cherokee, our clan had its own history and specific responsibilities which contributed to the well-being of the entire tribe.

Sometimes our family would walk together to the river for a special purpose; Grandma simply called it "going to the water." We would share a time of prayer and ceremony standing at the water's edge on a gravel bar beside the flowing stream. I didn't have a word for these special times when I was a child, but later I would call them holy and sacred. I would call them church.

My identity as both Native and Christian is forever inter-twined as I recall community rituals to honor those who had gone before. A processional of Cherokee people including Grandma would enter our family cemetery where tables and benches had been prepared. They came carrying traditional foods and singing Cherokee hymns. You could hear them singing as they came closer and circled the burial place of so many of our foremothers and forefathers. Following prayers and words of welcome, we would eat together beside the graves, telling stories from our past about those who made it possible for us to live in the present.

My Grandma spoke only the Cherokee language. Her voice was soft and musical. After I went to bed, I would listen to my Grandma and other women from our family visit together in our native language. The sounds reminded me of the lady sounds I would hear from the chicken house in the evening—the sounds of mother hens comforting their young. I was surrounded by the women folk, the men folk, the creatures of our world, and the sounds of the night. I had a place in the web of creation.

◆ ◆ ◆

These experiences brought me perhaps as close as I would ever come to an emotional connection with the precolonial life of my people. I have no doubt that before the arrival of European missionaries we knew Creator God and our Creator knew and claimed us.

The Indigenous Peoples of the world—those of us who have been forcibly separated from much of our culture, most of our language, our family, community and tribal structures, and the sacred element of our identity, which is the land, our Mother Earth—a great many of us have reached into our past and grasped a piece of who we were, are, and hope to be. The claiming of the truth that Creator God made us holy and beautiful, in God's own image, is a salvific and redemptive gift. Surely this must be one of the spiritual realities that Jesus Christ offers. When he told us to love God with all our being and our neighbors as ourselves, wasn't he telling us that it is essential to find the beauty and grace within ourselves in order to find it in others?

What Can We Learn from My Grandmother's Way of Leadership?

For the church of today and for the women and men who would offer themselves as leaders, here are a few possibilities of what we might learn from Grandmother's way of leadership.

- We can understand the importance of our female and male ancestors to our present life from our Indigenous communities. I think of Grandma, gone for decades, yet alive to me. Our connection with those who came before is essential to being who we are in the present.
- While kitchen culture is a place where women take part in quiet leadership and service, do not discount the wisdom, mentoring, and strength from which church leaders may draw and learn.
- Intergenerational life, learning, and relationships are great gifts for all. Children, young persons, adults, and elders are nourished by one another.
- Tribal hymns are a valuable part of our inheritance as Native American Christians and a valuable

contribution to the church and world. We still sing them in many Native churches. You may not understand the words, but the sound will connect you with Creator God. If your church is not close to a Native church, you can find recorded tribal hymns to share with your congregation by searching the internet.[1]

◆ Much Native American intergenerational teaching simply comes from observation, mentoring, and modeling of appropriate behavior expressed through a cultural worldview. This requires that elders and community/church leaders spend quality time with children and young people—not so much doing lessons as doing life.

Young Adult Memories of Wilma

Following the forced removals beginning in the 1830s known as Trails of Tears, many Native American nations found themselves relocated to different parts of Indian Country across the United States. For most nations, these were death marches, claiming the lives of many. My ancestors' designated lands of relocation were in northeastern Oklahoma. This land was held communally by the tribe. Despite the trauma of the forced removal, my people began to work together to recover, relying on the web of relationships and resilient family, community, and tribal structures that had enabled survival to that point in our history. Additionally, many of the tribes from the eastern and southeastern parts

---

1 An intertribal CD of tribal hymns is available from the Oklahoma Indian Missionary Conference. The cost is $10 with checks made out to OIMC, 602 SW 35th, OKC, OK 73109 or by Paypal on their website: www.umc-oimc.org.

of the United States had adopted Christianity in one of its many forms. There were many Methodists among the Cherokee, and there were instances of Methodist missionaries and preachers choosing to accompany congregations on their Trail of Tears, journeying with them to lands west of the Mississippi River.

Unfortunately, a series of federal laws was passed in the 1890s that resulted in great land loss and deterioration of the tribal way of life. These laws, starting with the General Allotment Act of 1887, empowered the US President to survey all Indian lands and divide them into individual allotments for individual Native Americans. Only those who accepted allotments and separated themselves from their tribes would be granted US citizenship. This federal action undercut the tribal structures, which served as social "safety nets" for the most vulnerable; led to tremendous opportunity for fraud among non-Native persons who coveted the allotments; and made the "excess" land following determination of individual allotments available for sale to white settlers. All of these things led to extreme poverty and alienation among tribal peoples in the decades following.

By the 1970s and 1980s many of my people living in rural parts of the Cherokee Nation struggled with some of the basic needs of life. One of these basic needs was access to clean water. Many in my family living in our part of rural Cherokee County continued to haul water or depend on hand-drawn water from wells that were no longer healthy. This, in turn, led to less-than-sanitary living conditions.

I was a young single parent working as a social worker for an urban Indian Health Service clinic. It was while visiting my Grandma that I first heard the name Wilma Mankiller. One of my uncles had recently retired, and he and my aunt were living close to Grandma, watching over her and help-ing with her care as she aged. He was the person who spoke to me of new happenings in the Cherokee Nation under the leadership of Wilma Mankiller, a young community devel-oper. The projects he was most excited about were rural water-line development projects, which were community empowering in nature. These projects were the result of community outreach, research, and relationship-build-ing, which grew from the work of Mankiller. She sought to address challenges faced by the community through a self-help approach. Additionally, this approach incorporated the rebuilding and strengthening of traditional community structures and relationships. Although there were many barriers, Mankiller persevered. Through her leadership and advocacy, rural water-line projects spread into many new communities. One of these was my community, known as Burnt Cabin. My uncle had worked for the water department of Oklahoma City for twenty-five years. He had worked as a general laborer for many years, but when he retired, he was one of the most knowledgeable persons on his crew. We felt Creator God had blessed us through the leadership of Wilma Mankiller, the know-how of my uncle, and the work of volunteers from our Burnt Cabin community. To this day, my family has running water because of the leadership and innovation of Wilma Mankiller.

Years later, after she became the first female Principal Chief of the Cherokee Nation,[2] I was honored to work for her administration and to become her friend. I continued to witness the strength of her leadership as a traditional

---

2   Wilma Mankiller and Michael Wallis, *Mankiller: A Chief and Her People* (New York: St. Martin's Press, 2000).

Cherokee woman and Indigenous Christian. One of my most vivid memories and proudest moments being a Cherokee clergywoman was officiating the wedding of Chief Wilma's daughter.

What Can We Learn from Wilma Mankiller's Way of Leadership?

For the church of today and for the women and men who would offer themselves as leaders, here are a few possibilities.

- Take risks to stand with Native women and Native Peoples on matters of social and racial justice.
- Explore the history of Christianity in regard to the Native Peoples in your conference. Consult your conference archives and remain diligent to examine both the positive and negative parts of history.
- Research the land history of your church. Trace how the land came to you and how Native Americans were involved. Use the information to write an accurate account and educate your congregation.
- Determine if your conference has held an Act of Repentance for Harm Done to Indigenous and Native American Persons. The 2012 General Conference mandated that all conferences of The United Methodist Church would hold such a service. If your conference has held an AOR service, acquire a video of the service for your congregation to view and discuss. If your conference has not held this service, arrange for representatives from your church to meet with your bishop and/or district superintendent to formulate a plan for moving forward on this vital action.

- If there are reservations, rural tribal entities, or urban areas with a Native American presence in your United Methodist conference, be intentional in your efforts to learn about their history. Find out from your conference leadership if there have been any relationships formed between these entities and your conference. Take action to ensure these relationships continue.
- Be in contact with your conference Committee on Native American Ministries to learn about activities and projects that are ongoing within your conference.[3]
- There are many insightful, well-researched biographies about Native American women leaders. Even if there are not Indigenous persons in your church or community, encourage and inspire others to learn about these Native leaders by obtaining some of these books and recommending/circulating them within your congregation.

Mid-Life Memories of Elouise

My family and much of my extended family continue to live on our land allotment, which we view as one way of connection with our ancestors and our Creator. My grandmothers and grandfathers were forced from original lands throughout the southeastern parts of the United States and onto our own Trails of Tears, which brought us to northeastern Oklahoma, where we now live. When I sit on the front porch of my home, feel the wind, and hear it rustling through the

---

3   For a list of CONAM Chairpersons and their contact information, go to the website of the Native American Comprehensive Plan of The UMC at www.nacp-umc.org.

trees . . . when I listen to the birds and cicadas sing in the evening, I feel the presence of my people, who suffered and sacrificed and whose blood continues to feed the earth that I might live.

◆ ◆ ◆

Throughout my life as a human being, a social worker, and a minister, I have witnessed a great many forms of racism and discrimination. I have witnessed corporate entities challenge the environmental rights of creation. I have joined community demonstrations when young Native Americans have been murdered with no follow-up law-enforcement investigation. I have supported Native American nations as they sought to preserve their right to clean water. As an Indigenous person from the Americas I have personally experienced racism from persons and institutions. Native Americans, in the context of US history, can easily come to believe the power of the institution always wins over the rights of human beings and creation. How healing it was to meet an Indigenous Christian woman who chose not to believe this was true.

It became a great experience of my life to meet and learn from Elouise Cobell. She was an intelligent, quiet woman, an accountant. Cobell was a member of the Blackfeet Confederacy and also served as their treasurer. In the course of her work she witnessed multiple incidences of failure on the part of the US government through the Bureau of Indian Affairs to effectively manage trust accounts and pay monies owed to Native Americans. Across the country, trust properties belonging to Native individuals and families were under the control of the Department of the Interior/Bureau of Indian Affairs. A great many of these trust properties were leased by the government to farmers, ranchers, oil and gas companies, and many others. The profits from these leases were to be paid to the Native owners. Cobell came to realize much mismanagement was occurring. Leases were granted at shockingly low rates. Monies were disappearing.

Elouise Cobell also witnessed the poverty and suffering of her people, and she could not look away. After trying and failing to draw attention to this economic injustice for many years, she decided to file a class-action lawsuit. This lawsuit required governmental accountability and reparations for Native Americans. Fourteen years later her lawsuit prevailed, and the US Congress passed the Claims Resolution Act of 2010, which provided repayment to individual Native Americans across the United States, returned many land parcels to communal tribal ownership, and established an educational fund, the Cobell Education Scholarship Fund for Native American and Alaska Native students.[4]

◆ ◆ ◆

The prophetic voices and actions of Native American women must be recognized and celebrated. Every day small, quiet actions and loud, rowdy actions of my Native sisters make it possible for our peoples to survive and to overcome injustice. I witness our elder women raising grandchildren and even great-grandchildren while parents struggle to remain employed while fighting addictions. I witness Native women

---

4   Bethany R. Berger, "Elouise Cobell: Bringing the United States to Account," in *Our Cause Will Ultimately Triumph: The Men and Women Who Preserved and Revitalized American Indian Sovereignty*, ed. T. A. Garrison (Durham, NC: Carolina Academic Press), 2014.

on our reservations and in urban and rural communities grapple with finding healing amidst the highest rate of violence toward women of any racial group in the United States. I witness our young Native women and girls struggle to overcome the highest rates of suicide for any age group in the world.[5]

Yet in the midst of this generational trauma, Indigenous women in the Americas and around the world are spinning gold from straw. The wicked burden of economic injustice is being challenged from the United Nations Permanent Forum on Indigenous Issues, where the voices of our women speak to the world—including to our Native American local churches where our women clergy and lay pastors lead congregations to live out their identities as followers of Jesus Christ.

What Can We Learn from Elouise Cobell's Way of Leadership?

For the church of today and for the women and men who would offer themselves as leaders, here are a few possibilities:

* Take on the Goliaths of our world, particularly economic injustice, a prime focus of the teaching of our brother, Jesus Christ.
* Be willing to walk long journeys to follow Jesus in challenging the powers and principalities of our day. Elouise Cobell entered her battle for the long haul—she worked for decades as an agent of change, and we must not give up or turn away from what Creator

---

5   Multiple sources may be found online for health/mental health data related to Native Americans and Alaska Natives. One I find helpful is the Substance Abuse and Mental Health Services Administration at www.samhsa.gov.

God calls us to do. Remember the long path that led to voting rights for women in our country.

◆ Find Native Americans and other Indigenous Peoples with whom to align in their fight for economic justice and other human rights. Remote technological access is available to us, particularly in the United States. Churches can research and reach out to support many Indigenous Peoples in our fight for human rights.

Current Memories of Future Lives

It is a morning several years ago. I awake and find myself with the warm, sleeping bodies of my two oldest grandchildren lying beside me. How did I come to be so blessed among women? They are my very young granddaughters, around the age I was in my oldest memories of my Cherokee grandmother. First one wakes and then the other. Their eyes are so lovely and graceful—full of the love, trust, and hope that flows between us. It is a singular moment in my memory. As I look into their eyes I feel the presence of my Grandma, and her Grandma, and on . . . and on. . . . As I look into their eyes, I feel the presence of their granddaughters, and their granddaughters, and on . . . and on. . . . I find the presence of Immanuel, God with us, in this cloud of witnesses—women and girls past, present, future. What am I called to do so that these souls filled with hope might be celebrating even greater accomplishments for women in one hundred years?

◆ ◆ ◆

This is the fourth voice I share with you—girl children of today and those yet unborn. I am called to be part of a church which not only walks with the girls yet to come but runs through time and space in order that their lives be filled with redemptive hope.

What Can We Learn as Leaders When We Consider Seven Generations Yet to Come?

For the church of today and for the women and men who would offer themselves as leaders, here are a few possibilities:

- If there are Native Americans in your community, whether or not you have Native Americans in your church, offer your facilities for activities that support Native life, such as Indigenous language classes and Native hymn singing.
- Be a presence at public Native American events in your community, clearly taking the role of respectful learner.
- Engage children and young people in your church to become connected with the lives and stories of Native American people. Strive to lead your church to model the formation of *relationships* with people who are different from yourselves.
- Become advocates of educational opportunities for Native young people in order to maximize the development of Indigenous leadership. Only 14% of Native Americans have college degrees, less than half of the rate among other groups in the United States.[6] Learn about tribal colleges and universities that are controlled and operated by Native American nations.

---

6   American Indian College Fund Report on Higher Education at www.collegefund.org.

In One Hundred Years

When we look at our babies, toddlers, and young girls of all ages and races, let us envision them in our minds, living lives of justice and peace—accomplishing great things with so many of the burdens of injustice lifted from their shoulders. Let us envision them walking with a sense of balance, even in turbulent times. See them loving Creator God with all their being and loving their neighbors as themselves.

Let us be the best church we can be as the eyes, hands, and feet of Jesus Christ. What we do today to eliminate racism, sexism, ageism, homophobia, and all forms of human bondage contributes to bringing about the wholistic circle of Creator God's vision for us. Let us rejoice for this hundredth anniversary of women's voting rights and be courageously working toward the continued transformation of humanity such that we give our granddaughters seven generations hence even greater reasons to celebrate!

Called by God but Misunderstood by the Church, Deacons Nevertheless Lead

*Rev. Victoria Rebeck, Deacon, Minnesota Annual
Conference, The United Methodist Church*

If you remove the yoke from among you,
   the pointing of the finger, the speaking of evil,
if you offer your food to the hungry
   and satisfy the needs of the afflicted,
then your light shall rise in the darkness
   and your gloom be like the noonday.
The Lord will guide you continually,
   and satisfy your needs in parched places,
   and make your bones strong;
and you shall be like a watered garden,
   like a spring of water,
   whose waters never fail.
Your ancient ruins shall be rebuilt;
   you shall raise up the foundations of many generations;
you shall be called the repairer of the breach,
   the restorer of streets to live in.

                    —Isaiah 58:9b-12 (NRSV)

Serving as a lay member of Northern Illinois Conference in 1997, I strolled among the displays during a break in the conference. At one table I learned something new: The United Methodist Church had an order of ministry it called deacon. In its description of how the ordained deacon has a distinct ministry (that is not preparation to become an elder), a sign on the table called to me.

Deacons:

- lead the church in relating the gathered life of Christians to their ministries in the world;
- interrelate worship in the gathered community with service to God in the world;
- create opportunities for others to enter into discipleship;
- connect the church with the needy, neglected, and marginalized among the children of God;
- contribute to worship and assist elders in administering the sacraments; and
- lead congregations in interpreting the needs and concerns and hopes of the world.

This was me. I was already living out the practice of this ministry.

Because I had a seminary degree, the senior pastor of my United Methodist church invited me to partner with him in leading an adult Sunday-school class. Outside of class, members and others turned to me with questions of faith and their struggles to practice God's love in a world fueled by greed and fear. I was already listening and guiding the faithful to find their ministries in the world. I had already been following inner promptings to start a food drive, assist in food pantries, learn about ministry alongside the urban poor, and sit in on challenging, frank conversations about racism and privilege. My call to connect the church among the needy, neglected, and marginalized has always been strong.

Yes, I was already engaged in these ministries, and this leads many United Methodist conference Boards of Ordained Ministry to ask, "Why do you need to be ordained?" It is one of the first obstacles thrown in the way of those called to the ordained diaconate. The question, though frequently asked of deacon candidates, reveals a broad lack of understanding across the connection about the meaning of ordination in The United Methodist Church. Looking at the Disciplinary paragraphs that describe the ministry of the elder, one can see that the church's primary perception of ordained ministry draws on function. The list of the elder's responsibilities is lengthy (and mentions quite a few ministries rightly assumed by the laity), and Boards of Ordained Ministry tend to gauge candidates' callings primarily by their capacity to perform these many tasks. Yet The United Methodist Church's ministry service ordinal demonstrates that acts of ministry are only a part of ordination. The ordinal's introduction constitutes what may be, at this point, the closest expression The United Methodist Church has of a theology of ordination.

Two central parts of the ordination liturgy are the same as they are for the baptismal covenant: the action of the Holy Spirit and the exchange of vows. Given that ordination has its foundation in baptism, this makes sense. The introduction tells us this:

> The sign of ordination, however, like baptism, should be understood not as a graduation, but as an initiation into the way of life of the order into which the candidates are being ordained. That way of life is governed by the vows attending each ordained

office. These vows, in turn, specify how these set-apart ministers, together with sisters and brothers in their order, are called and held accountable to live out their baptismal vocation within the life of the church for the sake of the world.[1]

Ordination is for "a lifetime of service," the introduction says. It "confers a new role in the life of the church as well as authority for leadership in specific forms of ministry."[2] Thus we are ordained not to be credentialed to "do" ministry—we have already received that through baptism. Through ordination, we enter into "a new role in the life of the church," with explicit accountability and responsibility to take leadership through our ministries.

I did not and do not take this lightly. I did not think that ordination was owed to me on the basis of what I had completed or attained or my sense of call. I gave it a lot of thought before I presented myself for ordination. I realized that the demands on the ordained deacon are no less than what they are on the ordained elder.

After ordination, I continued to minister in many of the ways I had before. However, I then had greater responsibility to the church and the world. I was more visible, carrying the authority and respect often granted to the ordained. I was responsible to step up to leadership—not only in an

---

1 "Services for the Ordering of Ministry in The United Methodist Church, 2017-2020," lines 244-50, https://www.umcdiscipleship .org/resources/services-for-ordering-of-ministry-in-the-united -methodist-church-2017-2020.

2 "Services for the Ordering of Ministry in The United Methodist Church, 2017-2020," lines 262-65, https://www.umcdiscipleship .org/resources/services-for-ordering-of-ministry-in-the-united -methodist-church-2017-2020.

appointment setting but beyond. My ordination requires me to take leadership in the community and the church structures beyond the congregation. Anywhere I go I must represent "the highest ideals of the Christian life," as The United Methodist Church's *Book of Discipline 2016* requires (¶ 304.2). Ordained deacons and elders all agree to this upon ordination. We have common areas of responsibility (Word and Service, for example), but we have distinctive areas of leadership. One way to look at these defining areas is to consider ministers of "sacrament and order" (elders) as having a primary charge to connect the gathered congregation to God. Ministers of "justice and compassion" (deacons) have a primary charge to connect the ministries of the baptized to the needs of the world outside the congregation.

Of course, there are exceptions in all these areas. The lines between the order of deacons and the order of elders are permeable, as they are with the ministry of the laity. We need not be rigid about this. Nonetheless, United Methodists should pursue a clear understanding about the distinct emphases of each order.

While not equivalent, the orders of elders and of deacons are not ranked hierarchically. However, many think of deacons as a lesser choice. "When are you going to be a real minister?" deacons are asked. Clergy mentors who are elders and district superintendents try to discourage those in candidacy or provisional membership toward deacon's ordination, "Don't you want guaranteed appointment? Don't you want more respect?"

Unfortunately, among those United Methodists who disrespect the ordained diaconate are some of the women elders who were among the first to gain clergy membership in The United Methodist Church. They, too, may suspect that women deacons have chosen "the mommy track," to pursue an "easier" call to ordained ministry. (Men deacons are discouraged by male and female church leaders as well for following a "lesser" path.)

We deacons admire and respect our older women elders and appreciate the obstacles they overcame and the determination it required for them to pursue ordination and persevere in difficult appointments. As we respect them, deacons ask for their respect in return. We recognize that women elders were belittled in attempts to block them from answering a call from God; likewise, we ask their support for our call that the church belittles, undervaluing the courage, vision, and risks it requires.

Another argument I have heard is that the ordained diaconate is secondary to the ordained presbyterate because deacons "have less education than elders." Deacons, like elders, must have master's degrees. (There are exceptions for elders and deacons after they pass a certain age.) Many candidates for deacon's orders earn a Master of Divinity, and some take the basic graduate theological studies in addition to the master's degree they already earned in another field. People in both orders complete what is deemed a master's degree. (I urge the church to avoid, however, making a classist argument that only those who can afford graduate education deserve to be ordained leaders.)

Like others exploring ordained ministry, I was encouraged to become a pastor. I am genuinely flattered that I had the confidence of so many who believed I had the leadership gifts for that role. I knew, however, that was not my calling. The idea and the nature of the work did not much inspire me. My heart was with those outside of the church, pushed to the edges of society. In general, the church in the United

States has been so inwardly focused on maintaining activities for its members that it has little energy left for speaking against injustice and binding the wounds of the overlooked and ignored. I experience a nudging to lead the faithful to walk from worship in the sanctuary into the neighborhood to build relationships with neighbors, especially those whom most churches are not wooing into membership.

My ministry is that of a deacon, and my identity is as well. Should the church ever decide to abandon the historic office of the deacon—which extends back to New Testament times—most of us who are deacons will remain true to our calling. We know ourselves to be deacons in our souls and in our relationship to God and the world. Speaking for myself, I know that I was given the gifts of the diaconate: a passion for justice for those who are ignored, belittled, or shunned; compassion for all who hurt; ability to guide the faithful to discover how God is calling them to reflect the light of Christ into the world; and the gifts to lead. I was created for diakonia.

As are my colleagues who are elders, I am connected to a congregation; I am not in ministry by myself. My ministry is to and with the people of God. I am also connected and accountable to others in the order of deacon. Unlike elders, I do not have the responsibility to order the life of the congregation and the denomination. Yet there have been ways in which I have contributed to ordering the life of a congregation and the greater United Methodist Church. I have helped congregations through significant decisions regarding their future. I have influenced the church to clarify at least a bit its understanding of the categories of ministry and how they work together. But overall, ordering the life of the church is not my primary calling.

Also unlike elders, I do not have the responsibility to provide the church access to its two sacraments of baptism and Communion. Unfortunately, many United Methodists, including many of its bishops, have adopted the phrase "sacramental privilege," implying that presiding is a right limited to few, at their own discretion. However, presiding is less a right than a responsibility. In a church that teaches its members that weekly (at least) Communion is the norm (see *This Holy Mystery*), elders are responsible for making sure it happens. Further, they have the responsibility to make sure that those entering the community of faith have access to baptism. I have a role in the sacraments, rising out of my representative ministry of the diakonia of all believers. I do not have the responsibility to make sure the faithful have access, because my ministry attention is focused outside the church walls.

Many sources (such as *The Book of Discipline*) teach that the word "deacon" comes from *diakonia*, a Greek root meaning "servant." Though lay people, elders, and deacons are called to ministries of service, it is the perception that deacons are servants that further reinforces the assumption that deacons are secondary to elders. (We must also keep in mind that Jesus taught us through word and example that those who serve others with humility are held in high esteem in the realm of God. Thus "servant" should not be seen by the church as inferior.) Nevertheless, "servant" may not constitute the full meaning of *diakonia*. Scholar John N. Collins[3] has extensively examined the word *diakonia* as it appears in Christian and other texts from 200 BC to AD 200. He found

---

3   John N. Collins, *Diakonia: Re-interpreting the Ancient Sources* (New York: Oxford University Press, 2009).

that in that period, the word was used to mean "messenger" or "emissary." It did not carry implications of humility or of helping the needy.

Scholar James M. Barnett points out in *The Diaconate: A Full and Equal Order* that the only use of the term "deacon" in the Bible that refers to a specific person is in Romans 16:1, wherein Phoebe is identified as a deacon. Popular understanding holds that the seven listed in Acts 6, who were assigned the task of distributing food to the widows in the Christian community, were the first deacons. However, Barnett points out, the text never identifies them as deacons.[4]

What to say about this—particularly given the church's long association of *diakonia* and its cognates with service? In the church's early years, deacons worked closely alongside bishops in a way that represented the office, much like an emissary. Eventually—still relatively early in the church's history—deacons also represented the church's ministry to the poor. In liturgy, this was demonstrated in the deacon's role of calling for and caring for the believers' donations to the alms collection.

I personally associate my sense of my own diaconal calling to both emissary and advocate for justice and compassion for the poor and marginalized. I believe these are both expressed in paragraph 328 of the United Methodist *Book of Discipline 2016*, which introduces the ministry of the deacon. In that paragraph, United Methodist deacons are charged to take leadership: the words "lead" and "leadership" appear six times. There the *Discipline* associates leadership with such duties as "connecting the church with the most needy,

---

4   James M. Barnett, *The Diaconate: A Full and Equal Order* (Valley Forge, PA: Trinity Press International, 1995), 158-59.

neglected, and marginalized among the children of God"; relating the gathered life of Christians to their ministries in the world; "teaching and proclaiming the Word"; "contributing to worship"; "assisting the elders in administering the sacraments"; "forming and nurturing disciples"; "conducting marriages and burying the dead'; "embodying the church's mission to the world"; and "leading congregations in interpreting the needs, concerns, and hopes of the world". As emissaries, deacons carry a message from the church to the world and from the world to the church. They advocate for justice and compassion, in this United Methodist description of the diaconate, through "embodying the church's mission to the world" and "connecting the church with the most needy, neglected, and marginalized among the children of God."

I practice my ministries of emissary and justice advocate in a number of ways. From 2013 through 2018, I served The United Methodist Church as the director of deacon ministry development at the General Board of Higher Education and Ministry. Through that work I supported and challenged deacons in their ministries. I particularly encouraged them to exercise leadership and continue to point the church back to the commandment to love its neighbors. In the many ways that I have been a writer and editor, I have drawn the church's attention to the most vulnerable and hurting.

I am a Minnesota Master Naturalist and a Tennessee Master Naturalist. Through these volunteer ministries I invite people to experience the Creator while in creation and engage in the spiritual practice of wonder. The more we learn about the complex diversity in creation as well as the ways in which all parts are inextricably interwoven, the more we will experience our part of creation with awe and, I hope, humility. My aim is to help people connect their spiritual practice of awe with a sense of responsibility to respect and protect all of God's creation. Contemplation and active compassion are two parts of the whole of discipleship.

I serve on the board of Tennessee Justice for Our Neighbors (TNJFON), a ministry supported by The United Methodist Church and other partners that provides affordable, high-quality immigration legal services to immigrants, educates the public and faith-based communities about issues related to immigration, and advocates for immigrant rights. I have demonstrated in support of continuing Deferred Action for Childhood Arrivals. I also volunteer at TNJFON's monthly legal clinics, where I perform intake interviews and talk with clients. Caring conversation with someone who is interested in their stories can be an important part of the agency's service.

In addition, from time to time I teach adult Sunday-school classes. I've taught about spiritual growth as well as issues facing The United Methodist Church.

The early Methodists met in groups where they talked about their faith practices and held each other accountable. I am part of a covenant discipleship group of women who meet weekly via telephone or an online meeting platform.

I am no different than other United Methodist deacons in that I experience my leadership in the church to be undervalued and misunderstood. As it does many deacons, this frustrates me. In the core of my self-understanding, however, I know that I was made a deacon. I have been given the gifts, the passion, the drive, and the willingness to take vows for the ministry. Nevertheless, through the grace of God, I lead.

As I write this, United Methodists are reeling from the contentious 2019 General Conference. As painful as it was, various groups within the church have begun to gather to talk together about what Methodism in America could look like in the twenty-first century. Some conversations are addressing not only the presenting issue of full inclusion of LGBTQAI+ Christians, but additional ways in which Methodists could be more faithful, Wesleyan representatives of the gospel.

The United Methodist Church began declining in membership long before 2019. Annual conferences have reacted by seeking younger candidates for elder's orders who would lead more energetic worship services that might attract more (young) visitors. This strategy aims to attract people to churches more than to develop disciples. At the same time, this raises another barrier put up against deacons: "We don't appoint deacons to . . . (new faith communities, multiple charges, etc.)." Many annual conferences keep deacons in a tightly closed box. In the meantime, the church desperately needs to return to its earliest commission to proclaim God's love to the world. While annual conferences continue to promote different musical preferences in worship in hopes that will bring life to the church, they turn their attention away from the world that finds the church increasingly insignificant.

The *Discipline* ¶ 328 says: "the ministry of the deacon is a faithful response of the mission of the Church meeting the emerging needs of the future." The church has always needed leaders who look to the future and address emerging needs. Intentional and strategic appointment of deacons can challenge the church to look beyond propping itself up as an institution and return to gathering and sending disciples of Jesus Christ who, in humility and compassion, reflect God's love to a hurting world. This is a *kairos* moment in the life of The United Methodist Church, as it discerns how and why it should exist. An intentional recruitment and empowerment of people called to the diaconate can help guide the church back to its calling. Not all may follow; the church may not become an institution with status in society. Faithfulness is represented more accurately through the lives of disciples than it is in the number of people who show up for worship.

Nevertheless—even though deacons are misunderstood and ignored—they persist in leadership. It may even be, in part, this experience of being devalued that gives them a heart for those overlooked by society. Deacons give urban children a vision for the wider world and their creative abilities when they help them keep a community garden. They show runaway gay teens, lost and exploited in the night, that God loves them as they are. Like John Wesley, they affirm and advocate for laborers. They guide prison inmates to know themselves and prepare for life on the outside. They hear the stories of the sad, the isolated, the frightened, the lonely. They speak up for the oppressed.

Deacons are builders of the realm of God; they persist in pursuing the vision of Isaiah:

> If you remove the yoke from among you,
>> the pointing of the finger, the speaking of evil,
> if you offer your food to the hungry
>> and satisfy the needs of the afflicted,
> then your light shall rise in the darkness
>> and your gloom be like the noonday.
> The LORD will guide you continually,
>> and satisfy your needs in parched places,
>> and make your bones strong;
> and you shall be like a watered garden,
>> like a spring of water,
>> whose waters never fail.

Your ancient ruins shall be rebuilt;
 you shall raise up the foundations of many
  generations;
you shall be called the repairer of the breach,
 the restorer of streets to live in.
—Isaiah 58:9b-12 (NRSV)